Contents

The Use of Military Force: Constants and New Trends
Professor Robert O'Neill
Chichele Professor of the History of War, All Souls College, Oxford;
Director, IISS, 1982–87

The Evolution and Future of Extended Nuclear Deterrence   18
Professor Lawrence Freedman
Professor of War Studies, King's College, University of London

The Logic of Strategy and the Upkeep of Extended Deterrence   32
Dr Edward N. Luttwak
Senior Fellow, Center for Strategic and International Studies, Georgetown University, Washington

The East–West Military Balance: Assessing Change   49
Simon Lunn
Defence Planning and Policy Division, NATO HQ, Brussels

An Unfavourable Situation: NATO and the Conventional Balance   72
Dr James A. Thomson
Vice President, RAND Corporation, Santa Monica, CA

Arms Control: Problems of Success   103
Professor Adam Roberts
Montague Burton Professor of International Relations, Oxford University

From Arms Control to Arms Reductions: Achievements and Perspectives   116
Ambassador Gerard C. Smith
Delegation Chief of US SALT I negotiations; Chairman of the Board, Arms Control Association, Washington

I've achieved a lot of things in my career that I didn't know I'd ever be able to. There's always that feeling of "I could've...., I should've...." I get a tremendous amount of pleasure out of my work. Sometimes work can replace complicated situations and life decisions that other people make. I feel working gives you a reason for life and makes one feel useful.

When I look back, it's hard to believe all that has happened in my life. I've set myself tasks and challenges, and sometimes it's been like a juggling act. There's nothing that I've said to myself I can't do. When I've set my mind on something I'd have determination and knuckle down, work at it, and study hard until I've achieved my goals, however long it takes.

My next challenge is to conquer the internet. I'm just about to buy myself a laptop and teach myself computer skills. Goodness knows how long this will take. There's one thing I'm sure of, one never stops learning. I guess this skill might take me for ever.

I've learnt to celebrate every day, why wait for your birthday? Celebration can be a daily activity; whatever brings you joy and happiness, be it your garden, something you've made or decorating a room, be grateful. After all, every day you wake up is a good day, and that alone should give you cause to celebrate. But it isn't bragging or boastful to celebrate your own achievements. I remember where I was a year ago, and toast the year ahead.

I've focussed on everything in life that gives me a feeling of wellbeing and pleasure, and where you really begin to fall in love with life and enjoy what you've got.

I regret not grasping an education with both hands when I had the chance (when I was young and at school). It wasn't entirely my fault with my family situations (both my parents worked hard to try and give us a better lifestyle). It makes me sad that they both died so young and never had the chance to see how well their children had done.

It's about the person you are, and if you're a certain type of person, I think you can achieve anything. You can be whatever you want to be or do whatever you want to do.

I'm a tough cookie because I had to be. My challenge was, I didn't have any qualifications. The fact that I'm still working now is something I'm so grateful for. There's no door you can't open. I had to choose between being a dancer, an athlete or a normal teenager, not bothering with boys or having a party going lifestyle. It was a day to decide: was it worth it? YES. When I stood behind the tabs in my adorable John Tiller Girls Line at the London Palladium waiting for the curtain to rise….. YES, it was worth it.

The Use of Military Force: Constant Factors and New Trends

PROFESSOR ROBERT O'NEILL

Introduction
WAR AS A FACTOR IN WORLD AFFAIRS
It would be impossible to count the number of conferences of the past century at which this subject has been examined. Almost always the perspective of the speakers has been to stress that war is extremely costly and becoming more so as weapons technology advances, that it is frequently counter-productive in terms of its long-term consequences for the initiator, and that it is downright immoral. Yet wars have gone on occurring, becoming more expensive, more destructive and staggeringly counter-productive, despite the wisdom in all the sermons preached against them.

Force has not yet disappeared as a way of settling disputes for two main reasons. First, for some it is the only means available for resolving a problem. Vietnam could see no way of dealing with the *Khmers Rouges* other than to give them a larger dose of their own medicine. Had Britain sought to get the Argentinians out of the Falklands by negotiation, they would be there still – and perhaps so would Galtieri. I am sure that President Reagan believes his use of force against Colonel Gaddafi was well and truly justified through both cause and effect. At the sub-national level there are countless examples that we can think of in which one of the groups involved in a dispute sees force as the only way to achieve its aims. Even the Anglican bishops at the recent Lambeth Conference seemed to be on the point of blessing such 'armed struggle' until they thought a little more about the plight of their brethren in Northern Ireland.

Second, many of those who initiate wars either do not understand what they are doing or fail to realize the size of the gamble that they are taking. They are not the kind of people to listen to academic or clerical discourse on this subject. Hitler would not even listen to his Chief of the General Staff in 1938. Kim Il-Sung could not have expected to be fighting the United States Eighth Army within three weeks of sending his own army across the 38th Parallel. Nor could he have thought for a moment about the difficulties of maintaining control over a peninsula whose coastline could be dominated by his enemies' overwhelming sea power. Saddam Hussein did not reckon on Iran having sufficient cohesion to rally and hurl his forces back within a relatively short space of time. Galtieri understood neither British nationalism nor the remaining capabilities of the Royal Navy in 1982.

So it is somewhat beside the point to list all the factors that make war an increasingly poor policy option. It has been such a poor policy option for a long time that, if those sorts of arguments weighed heavily in the minds of all those who can make war, it would have become entirely a matter for history professors a generation ago. I regret to say that – recent encouraging events in Afghanistan, the Gulf War, Angola and Korea notwithstanding – an academic monopoly of the subject still looks to be a long way off. War has not been outlawed, and nearly every state in the world maintains armed forces to use at its own discretion. With some 160 governments able to take decisions on whether or not to use their forces, it is naive to expect that all their choices will be either wise or moderate. Add to that the scores of sub-national and trans-national groups which have force at their disposal, and it is blindingly obvious that force remains a potent factor in world affairs for more active uses than deterrence.

My starting point therefore is that – for whatever reasons, wise or foolish – wars other than between the two super-powers and their allies will continue to occur. I do not think that I need to explain to this audience my reasons for believing that the super-powers will not clash directly as a matter of deliberate policy. But wars between other states, and within them, will involve the interests of external powers, great and not so great, and the most difficult problems that these conflicts will raise are whether or not to intervene, and if so, in what form and how far. They will also raise delicate dilemmas regarding stable conflict-management, the limitations to be observed voluntarily regarding the nature and extent of military operations, and the trade-off between interests in the particular troubled region and interests in the central East–West balance.

And all of us in this Institute are going to be involved one way or another as we always have been, but with the difference that, with thirty years of experience behind us, more will be expected from us than ever before. Those who work in foreign and defence ministries and serve in national armed forces will have to advise political leaders who, for the most part, will be very inexperienced in handling international security issues. The new breed of political leaders will have come up other ladders and will need comprehensive advice, or they might make the wrong move in a crisis. Legislators and those who comment on public policy matters will have to debate and pass judgment on complex government decisions relating to the use of force, decisions in which the public at large may not be very interested at the time when they are taken. Those who teach have a responsibility to prepare their students to cope with these kinds of problems, in theory and in practice, against the background of a changing world order. In fifteen or twenty years' time our security will be largely in the hands of today's graduate students. A chilling prospect! We theorists of course extend our hearts to the poor diplomats and service personnel who not only have to advise on policy but also must do something about it. While we sit at our word processors, they are out in the dust and heat of the theatre of war, or they are in the capitals of allied powers, listening sceptically to (or articulately enunciating reasons for) inaction, or they are enduring the *ennui* and street theatre at the United Nations, or they are waging that most taxing war of all: at the negotiating table. But one day, we all hope, they will receive their due in Nobel and other prizes.

The central problem: intervention in regional conflict
I intend in this Paper to focus on conflicts involving external intervention, because that is the most probable way in which most of us will be involved in thinking about the actual use of force. In the time available I neither can nor should add anything about the use of force between NATO and the Warsaw Pact. One of the few issues on which most members of the IISS are agreed is that we do not see how the use of force could be initiated in that context to any useful effect from anybody's perspective. In dealing with the Soviet leadership we are not facing inexpert or imprudent men. I shall not say that war between the two great alliances is impossible, for that is only to make it less so. But we do have more urgent issues to consider, so let me turn to them.

Obviously the nature of external intervention will change as both the local parties to a conflict and the interested external powers show that they have learned from past mistakes. Given the extensive experience of intervention that we now have available for analysis, we may expect the pace of learning, and hence of change, to accelerate. Indeed it has already done so during the past decade. There has been a clear trend towards less obtrusive intervention, with technical experts, advisers, intelligence information and war matériel substantially replacing external combat forces as the local parties become better armed and the political costs of supplying manpower from afar increase rapidly. As a result of this change there has been a swing in the balance of influence towards the local powers, creating new and increasingly difficult political situations for the external powers. But, although this may be a trend, it seems too early yet to say that major interventions by the forces of East or West will never occur again. Can we rule out that possibility in Korea, or in the Middle East? Is it entirely unthinkable in parts of Africa, the Caribbean, South Asia, South-east Asia or the Indian Ocean? While we may believe that limited conflicts involving intervention in those regions are less likely than they were twenty years ago, none of us can lay hand on heart and say we can forget about them as serious contingencies for study. Even less can we rule out intervention by regional great powers in conflicts on their own doorsteps. So what should we have learned from our long experience of this kind of conflict? What lessons can we derive to be applied in inevitably different circumstances and in rather different ways?

Some lessons well learned

There are several matters to be noted on the credit side of the ledger. Three lessons have been well learned. First, it is clear that the few powers which have nuclear weapons do not think that they are useful in regional conflicts and go to some pains to keep them free of any risk of involvement. Further, the nuclear great powers recognize the danger of escalation in any use of conventional weapons against each other and have learned to exercise restraint in operations which could lead to a direct collision. The oft-cited scenario of a world war being triggered by a regional conflict tends to be given too much credibility in public discussion. It is not impossible, but both sides have shown clear recognition of what is at stake in the past and have, on several occasions, demonstrated some skill in avoiding that final slide into chaos. That much progress has been made, erratically, painfully and not entirely by design, but it is there, pinned down, recorded and analysed in the classical studies on limited war and crisis management which are now part of the ground rules under which most major powers operate.

Second, we have come to understand from analysis of the crises of 1914 and 1938–9 that if the central strategic balance looks to be clearly uneven there is a very insidious destabilizing force at work. This is not so much the temptation the stronger power might feel to exploit his superiority as the fear of the weaker that he will fall further behind. We have learned not to be neurotic about the Warsaw Pact's possession of approximate strategic equivalence. We have also learned, in considering regional crises, not to expect stability in situations where the local balance is either very uneven or threatens to become so in the future. We do not expect flexibility in policy and strategy from a government which sees its future options as being even narrower than its present ones. The positive outcomes of the great crises of the nuclear era strengthen our confidence that we have made some progress in learning these kinds of lesson. The Berlin crises of 1948–9 and 1958–61, the Cold War climax of early 1951, and the Cuban missile crisis were severe tests which might have destroyed a weaker or less intelligently directed international system. Let us hope that the philosophies and strategies which guided the minds of policy-makers in those episodes remain in the forefront of the minds of all who make policy at a high level in the coming generation. Without a strong and stable central framework we may well find regional conflicts escalating into global crises.

Third, we have learned to seek stability through a balance of strength not only in aggregate but also in its component elements. Instability can result from an uneven political balance, even though the balance of military power may look to be in equilibrium. We think of security much more in integrated political-economic-social-military terms than we did a generation ago. We have also learned, from long negotiation at Panmunjom, Geneva, Paris, Camp David and elsewhere, that all these factors have to be taken into account in the design of stable settlements to disputes.

Some lessons not learned so well
POLITICAL OBJECTIVES AND POLITICAL LIMITING FACTORS
So much for confirmation of the major positive lessons learned in using force in the nuclear era. The negative lessons outweigh them by a wide margin. Let me begin by discussing political objectives. When was the last time that force was used in a major intervention by a Western power with the prior establishment of a well-thought-through political plan and set of goals? Certainly the spirit of civilian control of the military has been maintained, at least in the West. All too often, however, it has been upheld by a civilian leadership that constantly had to re-define its political goals in the light of military adversities which might have been avoided if clear political objectives had been thought through in the first place. Think of Korea in late 1950 and 1951. Think of Vietnam in 1967–8.

The political planning of a limited intervention needs to take into account not only the specific object, such as to repel an act of aggression, to forestall the collapse of a friendly government or to keep external enemies at greater distance from one's own borders. It has also to address four factors of a more general nature, and all the more easily overlooked because they are not always or often the problems that cry loudest for attention. First is the fostering of a sound indigenous political base. The French administration in Indochina scarcely bothered to address this problem until it was far too late, and the result was a much more difficult situation, not only for France but also for its successors in Indochina. In Korea, Syngman Rhee himself needed no fostering; that tough, wily old campaigner knew how to put a political organization together and how to keep control of it. But it was an autocracy, and when it ran out of steam – as one day it had to – there was nothing other than the Army to take its place. South Korea would have been better off if a greater American political effort had been devoted to the fostering of a successor generation.

Had the importance of this point really been grasped by the Truman or Eisenhower Administrations, it is difficult to believe that the subsequent American commitment to Vietnam could have been undertaken in the politically blinkered way that it was. What was needed was not just the US Military Assistance Command, Vietnam (MACV), but also the development of a Vietnamese structure of political power which could draw some real authority eventually from the people. Without such a political foundation, the work of MACV seemed bound to finish in frustration, because the United States, even if its own and the South Vietnamese armed forces had been militarily successful, could not have remained there for ever.

The Soviet Union, with all these examples of Western failure to profit by, could have been expected to have done far better in Afghanistan. Instead it tried to impose on the Afghan people a government composed of a particular faction of the Communist Party which was not only wildly out of touch with popular sentiment but also inflicted the deadly insult, in Afghan eyes, of being a foreign implantation.

Has anyone done better? Think of the British conduct of the Malayan Emergency. There was a clear recognition in Whitehall and at Westminster that Britain could not bear the burden of empire much longer, and, for much of the nine years between the outbreak of the Emergency and the granting of independence, a major effort was directed at working with the forces of Malay and Chinese nationalism to develop a durable, competent political system by which Malaya, and subsequently Malaysia, could be governed. We need to ponder much more deeply the conclusions to be drawn from this discussion for problems which are high on the international agenda today. In the case of Cambodia, what are we really doing to help build a viable alternative to Pol Pot? Are we merely making a rod for our own, and the Cambodian people's, backs? President Roh Tae Woo should be encouraged to continue walking along the path of internal liberalization that he has wisely taken. The United States should stop fooling about with the Contras. Politically, inside Nicaragua, they do not amount to anything. If there is no alternative to the Sandinistas in prospect, then that fact, however unpalatable, has to be accepted.

Second, an intervening power has to have a political strategy towards the enemy's government. All too often the tendency has been to disregard it until the military situation has reached such a stalemate that there can be no escape from negotiations. By that time the negotiations have to be carried through without the intervener being able to exert compelling military pressure towards compliance with his basic objectives. Think of Korea before the election of Eisenhower, with his inclination to get rid of the conflict by gambling on the credibility of a nuclear threat to China. During 1952 the war was costing the Democrats heavily in terms of popular support, and escalation could have damaged the Truman Administration even further. China and North Korea were just able to hold their own militarily and politically, refusing to compromise on the central issue of voluntary or compulsory repatriation of prisoners. I am not saying that it would have been easy to have elicited greater flexibility from China and North Korea earlier in the conflict, but it seems very doubtful that the gains achieved at the negotiating table were worth the agony of the last twenty-one months of the war. I do not believe that Truman and Acheson behaved unreasonably in formulating their policy towards China in 1950–51, but it is only fair to stand back at this point and look at its costs in order to learn from their experience. Treating an enemy as a pariah can have very expensive consequences.

Think of the Nixon Administration desperately trying to negotiate with a stubborn Hanoi government in the early 1970s, when it was perfectly obvious that the United States was on its way out of Vietnam, regardless of the military situation there. Perverse though it may sound, in limited conflicts the time for an intervening power to negotiate seriously is while the wind is still blowing a little in its favour, not when the enemy's confidence is rising, as Hanoi's was after seeing the consequences of the Tet Offensive in 1968. In a limited conflict an intervening power cannot bank on holding what it has indefinitely. It is not like a front line on one's own territory. Ironically, Vietnam may be about to pay the penalty of being too rigid over the future of Cambodia for too long and find itself with little leverage against a resurrected Pol Pot.

Third, intervention should be undertaken only after giving some thought to the international environment in which it is to be sustained. It is not enough to dress up a self-serving policy in grand ideological terms, as France did in Indo-China after the outbreak of the Korean War. If the cause does not meet with the approval of friendly governments and have potential for winning popular sympathy, continuing to support it will bring heavy costs, as the Johnson Administration discovered in its own agony in Vietnam. Of themselves, these costs are rarely compelling, but they reinforce domestic opposition, which ultimately can be decisive. These days, even the Soviet Union cannot flout international opinion without acute embarrassment, as its experience at the hands of the United Nations General Assembly proved during its Afghanistan invasion.

While intervention for blatantly selfish reasons is not yet impossible, its costs are rising, and international public opinion is becoming increasingly critical of such motivation. It does not appear to shun intervention in principle, of course, if one listens to the cries of the supporters of sanctions against South Africa. But anything smacking of the service of super-power interests is likely to attract howls of disapproval, and these have to be taken into account by policy-makers, particularly if there is a possibility that they could be committing themselves to a protracted engagement. The Reagan Administration was wise to ponder the international reaction to its Central American policies. Even with a brief intervention, such as the bombing of Libya, there are longer-term cost factors to be thought about – factors which can complicate the next occasion on which the use of force might be thought appropriate.

Fourth, and especially for Western governments, the power of domestic public opinion in the intervening country has to be addressed both in deciding to intervene and in planning operational strategy – particularly in a protracted commitment, where legislative approval of financial support is necessary. In the opening phase of a conflict, governments can usually count on public support for intervention if there is a clear wrong to be put right. Indeed Mrs Thatcher would have been excoriated had she shown anything other than robustness to General Galtieri. But spring and summer belligerence rarely survives the winter. Had the initial commitment of the British Task Force been indecisive and the conflict become protracted, the media and public opinion would surely have sounded a different note.

But those are the risks of democratic politics. The task of the political leader is to judge what he can swing public support behind and what he cannot. Taking refuge in passivity will not help him for long. Once public opinion is supportive, it has to be kept that way. Electors do not like spending money – let alone their relatives' or their own lives – on causes other than those which touch the security of their way of life and value system. Yet even less will they tolerate a leader who appears weak in the face of a serious threat to their nation's interests as they see them. This is as true of Russians as it is of Americans – except that the former can do less about it, at least in the short term. The maintenance of public support can be a very expensive business, consuming much of a politician's time, energy and political capital. But, if it is well done, there are great rewards in terms of reinforcing a leader's status in respect of other issues.

While political leaders cannot escape these dilemmas if a threat appears, they have to remember that what looks to their advisers and themselves to be a serious threat may well not seem so to a group of hard-boiled legislators or journalists, sceptical at best about the judgment and competence of the foreign-policy establishment. Further, there is nothing like a continuing foreign-policy crisis for giving the domestic opposition an opportunity to reverse the normal handicap of not having the status of the governing party. Suddenly very ordinary and unproven politicians can acquire an almost mystical status as campaigners for humanity and morality if the voters see the nation's efforts in a conflict as going for little effect.

An integrated political-military strategy
Those, then, are four major aspects that any government planning or considering an intervention should address in its thinking – preferably before deciding to make a commitment, but, if not before such a decision, then certainly after it. Next it must develop an integrated political-military strategy for realizing the aims of the operation in the theatre itself. It needs to be integrated because these commitments are never purely military in nature. Military action in these kinds of conflict carries political consequences of special importance. The traditional Clausewitzian approach of focusing on destruction of the enemy's armed force is just not adequate for this type of war, and it is sad to see how many skilled professionals do not see how inadequate it is. I am not saying, of course, that Clausewitz is inadequate, but not many people read the relevant parts of his work.

One of the most important lessons of the major conflicts of the post-1945 period is that the political goals frequently do not coincide at all with what one would expect the military goals to be. In Korea, after the armistice negotiations had begun in mid-1951, the most effective military goal was no longer to destroy the Chinese and North Korean forces but to inflict as heavy a relative cost as possible, so as to motivate both enemy governments to accept the United Nations Command terms. The Communist forces were worse off for equipment and supplies than for men, and thus their logistic system was a more important target than their front-line forces. The real cost to them of United Nations Command pressure on their front line was to be compelled to keep their logistic system as fully stocked as possible. They thus had to consume resources which were badly needed for the reconstruction of China, and which China could ill afford, in order to pull Kim Il-Sung's fat out of the fire. A well-stocked logistic system also offered more rewarding targets to a bombardment campaign directed specifically against it. Unfortunately it was not until well into 1952 that the United Nations Command perceived the rudiments of this approach and translated them into practice, particularly through the Air Pressure strategy.

In Vietnam, General Westmoreland initially focused his attention on the Viet Cong main force and then transferred it to the North Vietnamese Army, as it was committed increasingly to the war. One can readily see why he set these priorities. As Col. Harry Summers points out in his book *On Strategy: A Critical Analysis of the Vietnam War*, it was finally the North Vietnamese Army which defeated the South.[1] It was not the Viet Cong, because as a major armed force they had largely been consumed in the Tet Offensive and subsequent attacks in 1968-9. But this conclusion ignores much of the reason for the parlous condition of South Vietnam and why it could not stand alone against the North despite the huge amount of material assistance that the United States had provided since 1962. Had there been a real collective will in the South to resist both the Viet Cong and the North, it could have done much better than it did – perhaps not well enough to defeat the North, but that is no reason for not having tried harder to foster political cohesion. What was known as the Pacification Program did make serious efforts in this direction, but – as Ambassador Robert Komer, Chief Pacification Advisor to General Westmoreland from 1967, has written – from the outset even American civilians allowed the war to be looked at too much as a military problem.[2] It was not simply a matter of the military being politically blind. The political requirements of that war were so enormous that civilians well versed in politics tended not to see them as their responsibility.

A second lesson of these conflicts is that military and political strategies sometimes directly contradict each other. The simplest example that I can give is the dilemma facing a tank commander in pursuit of an enemy force. When he comes to the edge of a planted paddy field, should he drive straight on across it to close with his quarry, or should he drive around the edge and risk losing it? Military considerations urge him to go straight across; political considerations suggest that the political value of the rice in the field – or the political damage that would result from its destruction – is likely to be greater than the political gain of capturing a small group of guerrillas. Limited wars in developing and developed countries are replete with these types of situation. Most security measures have a political cost as well as a political gain, and the art of conducting this type of conflict is to be able to tell which is the greater. Such dilemmas confound Russians in Afghanistan, Cubans in Angola and Vietnamese in Cambodia just as much as they have confounded Western forces. They will continue to complicate the military and police operations of indigenous governments in all protracted struggles where long-term political allegiance is the object of contention. Anyone involved in the use of force in limited conflicts will have to have his own answers to these problems, or he will see his efforts go for naught.

Experience of counter-terrorist and peace-keeping operations in the past thirty years has demonstrated even more clearly than the larger limited wars the need for an integrated political-military strategy. Unless the political roots of terrorism and friction between neighbouring states are tackled, there will be no end to the violence that they engender. Such operations differ from those of limited warfare in that the military usually do not have to bear such a large part of the burden: the police and other state agencies can play a greater role, leaving the military to a somewhat more narrowly focused mission. These component forces will not understand their individual functions, nor avoid pitfalls that can complicate the tasks of the other agencies working with them, unless commanders and staffs have a good appreciation of the policy as a whole. The military may well be called upon to direct its implementation, particularly if the situation should deteriorate to the point at which the prevailing level of violence renders the other agencies ineffective.

Aspects of military strategy in limited conflicts
Enough of the political side of military action in limited conflicts. Let us not forget that military strategy and tactics, pure and simple, play important parts in such engagements. A subtle military approach will be seen as bluff if it is not based on high military competence. Soldiers need to be fit and disciplined, to be able to shoot straight and to be good tacticians. The gulf between the rich, free life of the young civilian and the harsher environment of his service contemporary has never been greater than today. There are limits to the amenities that can be offered to make service life more bearable, but exactly where they lie calls for judgment of a high order in middle and senior military ranks.

The sort of military action that does not involve suffering casualties exists only in the minds of woolly-headed fantasizers. As Clausewitz reminds us so compellingly:

The fact that slaughter is a horrifying spectacle must make us take war more seriously, but not provide an excuse for gradually blunting our swords in the name of humanity. Sooner or later someone will come along with a sharp sword and hack off our arms.[3]

Limited conflicts in developing countries involve slaughter just as much as those in Clausewitz's Europe. Clausewitz's stark imagery was justified almost to the letter by the Viet Cong retribution squads which sought to intercept deserters – or 'ralliers', as the South Vietnamese government preferred to call them – coming in to the northern perimeter of the Australian area of operations in 1966. Before killing those that they captured, they hacked off their hands and left them on top of the shallow graves as a warning to anyone who happened to pass by. War, when it comes, is no less brutal for being modern.

Yet in a protracted war it is casualties above all else which serve to reduce popular support within an external intervening power. People will not long tolerate the deaths of their sons or friends conscripted to fight in some peripheral conflict on the global chess-board. Nowhere have we seen this sensitivity to casualties more clearly than in the Israeli intervention in Lebanon. If it is a problem for Israelis in the face of the threats that they see on their own borders, we fool ourselves if we imagine that less-threatened societies do not react very adversely to significant losses in limited conflicts. Consequently, special care has to be taken to keep casualties to one's own forces low: the casualty equation in limited war is very different to that of an all-out struggle. It is nonsense to compare body counts as if a one-for-one ratio was an acceptable trade. One must look more deeply at the relative political and economic costs of casualties to both sides before loss comparisons can have any meaning. The evaluation of the costs and gains of operational methods must reflect this wider calculus. It reveals very succinctly why the United States, its allies and the South Vietnamese were defeated.

A second way to lose political support for a commitment is to allow commanders high ammunition consumption rates, particularly of the more sophisticated and expensive ordnance. There is something very naturally reassuring in blazing away in the general direction of the enemy, and, if he is not to be seen, then all the more ordnance is needed to produce a satisfying effect. But extravagant use of ammunition is extremely expensive. It looks bad and can easily smack to the media of panic. It invites ridicule. It encourages prodigality in other areas of operational expenditure and leaves the government with an increasingly difficult task when it comes to prising financial approval out of the legislature. And the most uneconomic use of ammunition is generally the least effective. I can think of nothing more wasteful than the B-52s that used to fly from Guam, 2,500 miles away, to their targets in South Vietnam, dropping 500-lb bombs into jungle where the result could not be assessed and where, if one was forty or fifty yards from the point of impact, one had a remarkably good chance of surviving. I recall being on duty one morning in the battalion command post when an unfamiliar but highly indignant voice came through on the command net. 'What the f*** is going on?,' it demanded. The speaker was the American commander of a South Vietnamese special reconnaissance patrol which had unwittingly found itself in the target zone of a nearby B-52 raid. He was not reassured by the reply but, resourceful man that he was, he took his patrol to ground, and, an hour after the bombs had stopped falling, out of the jungle they all marched. A few had bleeding ears but otherwise they seemed little the worse for their misadventure. High explosive is a fine way to destroy a target when delivered with precision. It is also very effective against massed attacks in the open. It offers good value when the worth to the enemy of the target destroyed, in relative terms, exceeds the total cost of delivery. Otherwise it is a very expensive delusion in any kind of war. It is particularly regrettable that the lessons of aerial bombardment, so slowly learned in the Korean War, were relearned even more slowly in Vietnam.

Knowing and outwitting the enemy
Victories are usually not won simply by the bravery and skill of the men on the winning side. Their success has to be founded on an earlier battle of wits between the opposing commanders. One of the scarcest commodities in this contest is knowledge of enemy strengths and intentions. In conflicts in remote and unfamiliar places, with or between indigenous forces, the difficulties for an intervening power are extraordinary. All too often, the situation for the enemy is the opposite, because an external intervener is so visible and tends to care less about security of information than his enemy, who has survived because he is accomplished in the clandestine arts. An intervener begins with a poorly stocked data base. The opposing commanders are not known, the organizations and capabilities of his forces are only sketchily understood, and there is great uncertainty as to how much assistance he is likely to receive from other sources. All this information usually has to be built up while operations are in full swing. Hence there is a high risk of early disasters. Gradually the heat of action will dispel some of the fog, but what remains can be formidably dense.

The basic problem is to build a system of sources. In most of these conflicts satellite reconnaissance does not help very much, and scope for signals intelligence is limited. The key source is people – indigenous people. But why should they be helpful? Why should they accept the risks inevitably involved in this kind of work? Frequently it is because they are already alienated from an enemy whom they fear, or else because they want to make some money out of the conflict. These are hardly motivations which lead to objective reporting. But the picture is usually not entirely bleak. There will be some intelligent and honourably motivated people to whom one can turn if the cause for which one is working has any local support, but it takes time to find and train them. It takes skill and trust to be able to use and retain their services. Without indigenous sources, the intelligence task is hopeless. And when confidence is low, Gresham's Law applies in information every bit as much as in finance. It is amazing who is listened to in those circumstances.

It is one thing to obtain useful information; it is another to use it wisely. It is very difficult for any intelligence analysts to put themselves in the enemy's place and interpret material according to his operational codes rather than their own, and the wider the cultural gap, the more difficult it is. An intervening power is fortunate if it can call on its own citizens or on allies with long-standing expertise from colonial or other experience in regions of interest. But it is not always easy for the allies to help, much as they might like to.

One of the most besetting sins in the interpretation of intelligence is the tendency to slant analyses to favour the operational preference of the analyst. Intelligence officers have to discipline themselves to stay out of the policy controversies which tend to rage within operations staffs. Otherwise their judgment will become distorted, and their commander will no longer have the benefit of much objectivity in the information on which his operations staff is working. The other side of this coin is represented by the operations staff officer who has rigid preconceptions about what intelligence is significant and simply ignores what does not suit them. It takes a very perceptive commander both to detect this state of affairs and to be immune from such prejudices himself. General Westmoreland's headquarters suffered badly from these problems in the mid-1960s.

An integrated command structure
Good intelligence and operational planning will not achieve a great deal unless there is an effective command system linking indigenous forces and external assistance, whether that assistance is in the form of operational forces or, as is more likely today, advisers, specialized units and logistic support. The days of placing the indigenous forces firmly under an external power's commander, as in Korea or in Cambodia under the Vietnamese, are running out. The authority of the external power is much more circumscribed than twenty years ago, and the risks of the intervention miscarrying are higher. But, by the same token, the ease of extrication is now greater if the commitment has to be written off. The worst of all worlds is the situation which prevailed in the Vietnam War, when nobody was in charge, and indigenous and external forces fought separate engagements and conducted different policies.

Limited conflicts and the media
Limited conflicts, especially those involving external powers, arouse intense media attention and require a special media policy to be devel-

oped by the command authorities. Rarely are conflicts as remotely situated, speedily concluded and easily isolated from the media, as was the Falklands war. British media policy in that conflict, however well it obviated many of the problems which confronted the US in Vietnam, can scarcely serve as a model for external powers in other conflicts. Media representatives will usually be on the scene and impossible to control very closely. If they are not to become a wholly negative factor in the public debate on a particular conflict they need to be convinced that the strategy being applied is correct and that the results achieved are justifying the cost of the support provided. To retain the active interest of the more expert journalists in the aims of the commitment itself, rather than in tearing it to pieces, governments must give them some insights into the real dilemmas of command and operations. There are, of course, security problems in so doing, but if the media do not see an intelligent plan being put into effect with a degree of skill, and a justifiable measure of success in the light of the costs suffered, they are likely to complicate severely a government's task in maintaining popular support for a commitment. They will transform dull, unconvincing briefings into their own form of theatre, as we saw with their treatment of the Joint US Public Affairs Office (JUSPAO) during the Vietnam War. Commanders at most levels need to be able to talk with some frankness to the media and they have to be educated in so doing. Feeding the media on pap in a limited conflict is, in effect, providing a major dividend for the enemy.

In conclusion
One of the problems we face in analysing how force might be used is that many new nations and other groups have become exponents of war in the past forty years. We may have learned that central strategic war between East and West is not a feasible option, but we are very far from learning that same lesson with respect to regional and national conflict. Important changes are occurring, as developing countries become the arbiters of their own security to a greater extent, and as the developed find military intervention increasingly expensive in relation to what security or influence it yields. Force may yet remain one of the important currencies of international intercourse, but its value is depreciating. Good human common sense can take part of the credit. So also can the relative stability of the central balance over the past forty years.

But we are not out of the wood yet, either in regional or in global terms. Regional stability must be built through regional co-operation. For a very long time, global stability will still depend on the steady management of great power rivalries, while regional powers and sub-national groups continue to rock the structure by using force on each other. The inter-relationship between the central balance and the warring regions seems likely to continue to be the most challenging problem where the actual use of force in the world is concerned. While it is far from easy to see how regional conflict can tip the super-powers over into a wider war, it is not difficult to see that they will feel that their interests are involved in every significant regional conflict around the world. They will find it difficult to avoid becoming involved in supporting one or another of the participants. Intervention, be it direct or indirect, will remain the key concern for applied strategists.

We, as analysts, need to pay it more attention. Those who are the practitioners have a formidable challenge to master. They will need all the help that thinkers can offer. I wonder if, in thirty years' time, the Institute will be able to feel as proud of its contribution to the strategy and control of limited conflict as it can of its contributions to the study of the stable management of the central balance over its first thirty years.

Notes

[1] Col. Harry G. Summers, Jr. *On Strategy: A Critical Analysis of the Vietnam War* (Novato, CA: Presidio Press, 1982), p. 84.
[2] In his book *Bureaucracy at War: US Performance in the Vietnam Conflict* (Boulder, CO: Westview Press, 1986), p. 5.
[3] Clausewitz (trans. Peter Paret and Michael Howard) *On War* (Princeton NJ: Princeton UP, 1976), p. 260.

The Evolution and Future of Extended Nuclear Deterrence

PROFESSOR LAWRENCE FREEDMAN

No aspect of the nuclear dilemma has been more fruitful of plans and programs, of issues and controversies, in military strategy and arms control policy, than extended nuclear deterrence.[1]

Introduction
Extended deterrence has frustrated the strategic studies community for three decades by posing questions that it ought to be able to answer but cannot. The most difficult question of all is to what extent the issue really matters. Deterring aggression by the Warsaw Pact – conventional or nuclear – has turned out to be easier in practice than it ought to be in theory. This is perplexing to the theorists. To the practitioners it can also be perplexing, for without a theory how can they be sure exactly what it is that they are doing right?

The theorists of course are not short of answers to the central questions of extended deterrence, and some find their answers more than satisfactory and even campaign on their behalf. However the strategic studies community – let alone the wider political community – as a whole has not rallied behind a single set of answers. The central questions are:

- How can the United States use nuclear weapons to gain a decisive strategic advantage without running the risk of devastating retaliation?
- Without a satisfactory answer to this question, how can the United States sustain the commitments made to allies to use nuclear weapons on their behalf, should the need arise?

There would seem to be a close logical connection between these two questions, so that apparent failure to devise a credible nuclear strategy might have been expected to have undermined Alliance cohesion. Yet, while this failure has proved awkward for NATO, it has not proved fatal.

Nor has this failure inhibited continuing a debate surrounding extended deterrence. Indeed the debate has become part of Alliance ritual. Sometimes it serves as a coded means of talking about the distinctive security interests within the Alliance without sounding too blunt; more often it just provides the best theory available to guide the developments of force plans and doctrine. The categories with which strategy is discussed in the West have been forged through this debate.

So much has it shaped our language and thought that we take for granted that there is a real problem at its core, and that the problem has been properly defined, even if its solution still eludes us.

The extent of the cover provided by the US nuclear umbrella remains insoluble in analytical terms. The idea of extended deterrence is rarely dissected or defined with precision. Yet within NATO the term is immediately recognized to refer to the complex of measures considered necessary to reassure Western Europe that the United States understands its nuclear obligations. Familiarity has turned the term into a convenient shorthand. But simplifying complex relationships risks simplifying the problems of policy. Once it is assumed that Alliance cohesion is dependent on one central factor, then anything which affects that factor can threaten a crisis within the Alliance.

NATO's theory
Behind the anxiety over extended nuclear deterrence (END) are two key propositions. First, the quality of the deterrent threat depends on the ability to implement it, should deterrence fail. This problem is considered to be particularly acute, given that NATO is dependent on the threat of first nuclear use. Second, stable nuclear deterrence – mutual assured destruction (MAD) – at the super-power level undermines extended nuclear deterrence by undermining the credibility of the first-use threat. (Thus MAD is mad because it will mean the end of END.) Strategic instability at the centre is assumed to generate strategic, and in consequence political, instability at the periphery.

SOURCE OF DETERRENCE
The first of these propositions is at the centre of the professional strategic debate. It is also the easiest to dismiss. The flaw is in confusing (adapting Patrick Morgan's distinction) *immediate* with *general* deterrence.[2] Immediate deterrence involves an active effort to deter in the course of a crisis, when the efficiency of any threats will soon be revealed in adversary behaviour. General deterrence is altogether more relaxed, requiring the conveyance of a sense of risk to a potential adversary to ensure that active hostilities are never seriously considered. General deterrence might be considered as a condition which requires only moderate attention to be sustained; immediate deterrence is less a condition than a strategy to be adopted at a time of crisis.

There is an urgency to immediate deterrence which can be recognized in the government papers of the late 1930s, or the late 1940s. It can be detected in the 1950 document NSC-68 and the identification of a 'year of maximum peril' in 1954. When 1954 came, and the peril appeared manageable, there was a deliberate shift to a preparation for the 'long haul'. That was the point of transition from immediate to general deterrence.

This distinction could help NATO come to terms with the limitations of Flexible Response. Of course many in the NATO establishment believe that this doctrine offers useful guidance in the event of sustained Warsaw Pact aggression. But in practice 'flexible response' is satisfactory only as a peace-time doctrine, offering a form of words that can accommodate the great variety of strategic perspectives found within the Alliance. In current circumstances this is exactly what is needed; it may be a necessary myth to pretend that it would serve so well in the highly charged circumstances of war.

It works in peacetime precisely because it does not prescribe for actual hostilities. The language of flexibility and options avoids confronting the dilemmas of coalition warfare. It postpones the most difficult of all strategic decisions to a hypothetical time when they could be postponed no longer but when they could also at least be made by reference to the developing political and military context.

Once extended nuclear deterrence is discussed as an immediate challenge then it soon appears difficult and even hopeless. There is now a substantial literature which draws on the history of international relations and points to the difficulty of manipulating threats to influence an adversary's behaviour.[3] What is put into these threats is rarely what is received. Examples can be found of misunderstandings and confusion which either fail to deter someone who needs deterring, or else aggravate a crisis that might have otherwise been managed peacefully. Military signals in particular are often notoriously ambiguous, and the problems of interpretation grow in the psychological intensity of crisis. Even if threats can be well constructed and are perfectly understood when a conflict reaches crisis point, they are still only one part of the equation: the interests at stake, the underlying political trends, the attitude of allies and so on must also be considered. The specifics of the adversary's conduct constitute only one variable among many, and not necessarily the most important.

The problem of immediate extended nuclear deterrence is addressed by speculating on the specifics of a future East–West confrontation and wondering how on earth the West will cope. The starting point is the failure of deterrence and the fear that, unless one has something sensible to do should it fail, then it is no more than bluff. Eventually it will be exposed as such, and so deterrence will fail. But that assumes that the success of general deterrence depends on a speculative assessment of performance against the far more demanding criteria of immediate deterrence. There must be some link between the two but it need not necessarily be as close as is often assumed.

The possibility of catastrophic miscalculation by either side casts doubt on the validity of a strategy of immediate deterrence in an intense crisis. However, this same possibility if anything reinforces general deterrence, in that it reinforces a disinclination to war. Both types work, if at all, through the adversary recognizing an unacceptable risk of incurring unacceptable costs for inadequate gain – but in the immediate version this must be a complex calculation, while in the general version all that is needed is a vague feeling that certain options are just not worth pursuing. Nuclear war, even if the worst excesses of city-busting and 'nuclear winter' can be avoided, will be so horrific that only the most extreme political pressure would make it worth tolerating the slightest risk of its coming to pass. So long as there is a measurable risk that a confrontation could end up with nuclear detonations there is every incentive to avoid the confrontation.

This residual risk saved nuclear deterrence once the preferred approach based on a clear-cut superiority, no longer seemed to be plausible. There is no strategic formula to prescribe what is necessary to sustain this risk. It is about tolerating processes of great potential irrationality which create the chance of nuclear weapons being detonated. Circumstances discussed in the literature include a desperate and intense conventional fight in which passions have been raised, rash decisions become more likely and the overall situation slips out of control, and/or some catastrophic series of accidents leading to nuclear weapons being launched when better information and control would have made this wholly impossible.

Recent ideas about 'existential deterrence', according to which the mere possibility that nuclear weapons could be used creates a sufficient deterrent effect,[4] have an intuitive strength largely because we are aware of conflicts where reckless and terrible deeds have been done by people/states who would not have believed themselves capable of such things beforehand. The uncertainties and pressures of war cast doubt on attempts to construct doctrines for nuclear use, and so in turn make it extremely difficult to rely on such doctrines as a basis for reliable deterrent threats. By the same token, they give sufficient credibility to deterrence based on the prospect of a confrontation getting out of control and disaster through inadvertence.

As confidence in the possibility of constructing a deterrent threat based on a credible war-fighting posture began to decline in the late 1950s, increasing stress was placed on stabilizing the balance as a positive good: largely by removing any reason to fear a first strike, improving command and control procedures, introducing the 'hot line', and other forms of crisis communications. More recently there have been arguments for making it even more difficult to use nuclear weapons by tightening up on procedures for release, by reducing the role of the weapons in war plans and through regular affirmations by Presidents that 'there can be no winners in a nuclear war'. There have been proposals to make peacetime promises of 'no first use' and to remove those weapons (mainly short-range) from deployments where they might get caught up in a conventional battle. There is no evidence that the tendencies in this direction are less strong in Europe than in the United States, although there is a clear body of opinion that remains uncomfortable with the implications.

The more that the potential for the loss of control or inadvertent disaster is reduced as a deliberate – and wholly understandable – objective of policy, the lower the credibility of existential deterrence. Thus extended deterrence might be able to cope with a stable balance, so long as it is not too stable, on the grounds that any likelihood that nuclear weapons would be dragged into any serious war suffices to deter. Could it cope with a super-stable balance?

CORE AND PERIPHERY

Before we attempt to answer that question, we need to return to the second proposition behind extended deterrence – that stability at the core leads to instability at the periphery. The super-powers cannot be expected to run the risks of nuclear war in support of peripheral interests. States of peripheral interest to their super-power ally but of core interest to their super-power adversary clearly have problems.

The question of what constitutes a 'vital' interest is critical here. The discussion of this question in US policy-making circles from the start of the Cold War has been over how far the concept of vital interests can be extended to ensure a link with nuclear deterrence. This could be seen even with the Carter Doctrine of 1980. The experience of SEATO and CENTO suggests that merely to declare alliance is not enough, and that policy-makers make distinctions about the risks they are prepared to run and the resources they are prepared to devote to different regions of the world. Western Europe, Japan and South Korea rate higher than other regions. To some extent this is a reflection of historical and institutional reasons as much as an analysis of objective interests. The argument became muddied by such notions as the 'interdependence of commitments'. However, there was an awareness of the limits to which deterrence could be extended, and that these limits were a function less of the strategic balance itself (especially once the US lost any semblance of superiority) as of the definition of vital interests.

There is no evidence that with the growth of 'stability' the core has shrunk and the periphery grown in a mechanical fashion. For example, it was assumed by many in the 1950s that the cohesion of the Western Alliance depended on the United States retaining a measure of superiority over the Soviet Union. Those who looked forward to consolidating the developing strategic stalemate on the grounds of its stability were warned that a stalemate would make it far less likely that the United States would be able to provide credible security guarantees to its allies. Many in the allied states agreed. The United Kingdom and West Germany sensed increasing difficulty in persuading the United States to continue with the robust doctrine of nuclear deterrence developed in the 1950s. De Gaulle argued that nuclear alliances were untenable and that unavoidable doubts over the US guarantee meant that self-respecting states would have to look to their own (nuclear) devices to obtain security.

Yet, contrary to these expectations, the consolidation of super-power strategic stability during the 1960s, celebrated as mutual assured destruction, was coincident with the consolidation of political stability in Europe. The conclusions drawn – admittedly not immediately – from the Berlin and Cuban crises of 1961 and 1962 was that the major powers were highly reluctant to run any risk of nuclear war and that this required tolerating the *status quo.*

Equally, as members of the strategic studies community became gloomy about trends in the US–Soviet balance during the 1970s, dire consequences were predicted on the grounds that the Soviet Union was developing a range of nuclear options that the United States lacked and which might even allow them to undermine Presidential resolve in a crisis. There was to be a window of opportunity for the Soviet Union in the 1980s. In strictly technical terms, US military policy failed to close this window; yet the Soviet Union demonstrated no great sense of opportunity.

The reason for this is not hard to discern. The military postures of the major powers are one of a number of factors which shape the current security system. At some times these postures are more important than at others. Then they have to be fashioned carefully with regard to political positions: this is what strategy should be about. But the political variables are more critical than the military ones. The theoretical problem at the heart of the debate on extended deterrence has not yet become critical in practice because the political context has not obliged political leaders to address the stark choices posed. Deterrence has been practiced at the general level but not really at the immediate, with the possible exceptions of the early stages of the Cold War, when the current security system was established, and the Berlin and Cuban missile crises.

The relationship between extended deterrence and vital interests is in some ways circular. Extended deterrence acknowledges the possibility of becoming caught up in a total war as a result of commitments made to another country. If that possibility is significant, then by definition the security of that country has become a vital interest. Hence the focus within the Alliance on creating possibilities for a local conflict to escalate to a super-power level. The possibility of military instability creates the conditions for political stability.

Extended versus central deterrence
This brings us to the problem of the relationship between extended and central deterrence. These are often described as distinct types. While they share a number of fundamental features, especially the belief that an adversary's aggressive inclination can be controlled through threats, the character of the threats involved are quite different, and possibly even contradictory.[5]

Thus extended deterrence appears much more difficult than central deterrence. The American homeland is only really vulnerable to nuclear attack, and to deter such an attack all that is needed is the threat of nuclear retaliation in kind. This is credible because attacks on sovereign territory – the most vital of all vital interests – are considered to provide sufficient motivation to order a nuclear riposte.

With extended deterrence, on the other hand, it is necessary to be prepared to launch a nuclear attack in response to a conventional attack against third parties. This strains credibility.

The Alliance tensions caught in the notion of extended deterrence are illuminated by views concerning the point at which deterrence can truly be said to have failed. At most points during the course of a war one can imagine how things might still get worse, and so deterrence can be applied once war is under way. For the US, the priorities within deterrence might well be to concentrate on preventing a war either 'going nuclear' at all or at least expanding beyond the combat zone. Europeans on the other hand may feel that deterrence has failed once Europe becomes in any sense a battlefield. This of course leads into the classic problem with designing a force structure appropriate to extended deterrence – will the US try harder or less hard on behalf of Europe if it feels it can protect its own homeland?

Yet the possibility of a threat, nuclear or otherwise, to the US only arises in the first place because of its overseas commitments. If the United States were being truly isolationist, almost by definition it need not clash with any other power. Once the United States decides not to be indifferent to what is going on in the rest of the world, it is obliged to accept the risks that come with engagement. It is true that an isolationist United States would also want a nuclear arsenal to ward off any hostile powers – at the start of the atomic age this potential was seen by many adherents of the new weapons to be their greatest virtue. However, it is highly unlikely that a nuclear arsenal developed for this purpose would be assessed against the same sort of exacting standards that have in practice been adopted by the United States over the past decades.

It may therefore be the case that there is no serious requirement to deter a direct challenge to the United States. If the United States is under a threat, this is because it is intimately involved in the affairs of other regions. Capabilities to attack the United States might exist, but it is only the extension of American interests that creates potential conflicts with other powers.

Central deterrence therefore became necessary because of Alliance commitments. The greater the vulnerability of the United States the less likely it has appeared that it would take risks on behalf of allies. The problem of vulnerability would be most acute if the United States could be disarmed in a surprise attack. Despite preoccupations with the survivability of land-based ICBM and suchlike, this fear has, to all intents and purposes, been abated. For exactly the same reasons, the United States cannot protect itself against Soviet retaliation should it initiate nuclear hostilities. This is why the problem of extended deterrence has now narrowed down to the credibility of a first-use threat.

Thus, rather than being a distinct type of deterrence, extended deterrence may be better understood as an attempt to achieve the maximum deterrent effect from a particular strategic relationship. In this sense, one might just as usefully describe central deterrence as contracted deterrence, to indicate shrunken political objectives, or previously 'vital' interests being consigned to the periphery. It is hard not to have some sympathy for the view that the qualifier 'extended' is superfluous. Governments attempt to deter in support of national interests. At issue is the extension not of deterrence but of national interests.

Alliance and deterrence

Joining any peacetime alliance can be said to be an act of extended deterrence, since it involves making a commitment to go to war if another is attacked by a common adversary, in the hope that, as a result of this commitment, the adversary will be deterred. However, states joining alliances often do so less because they are expecting to go to the aid of others than because they hope that others will come to their aid. The connotation of extended deterrence is of weak powers drawing upon the strength of a great power, even though the great power itself may not be directly at risk. To explore the peculiarities of extended deterrence it might be useful to discuss it in terms of a crude framework of alliance relationships.

We can define two ideal types of alliance: symmetric and asymmetric. In symmetric alliances the power resources at the disposal of the individual members will be broadly equal. In asymmetric alliances the distribution of power is uneven, and one state is pre-eminent. In both types the cohesion of the alliance depends on the shared sense of threat and the confidence that the aggregate military strength exceeds that of the adversary. If neither condition is met, then there is a risk that individual members will peel off because they do not consider the *direct* threat to their own security to be significant, or because they lack confidence in the alliance's aggregate military strength and judge that they might be better off in an alternative arrangement, perhaps involving a degree of accommodation with the adversary.

A state's sense of a direct threat depends not only on its perceptions of adversary intentions, but also on the extent to which it acknowledges an interest in the security of its partners. At one extreme we might find a shared history and values, or a common geopolitical fate; at the other, states which, for different reasons, have an enemy in common but little else. The distinction might be described as one between a '*positive*' and a '*negative*' alliance: that is, one based on a broad political community, and one that is little more than an expedient response to a sense of threat.

A symmetric alliance might be expected to be driven most of all by the shared sense of a common threat. An asymmetric alliance, in which the strongest member may have no reason to feel directly threatened, may need to be more positive, involving a clear sense of how great-power interests are bound up with the fate of smaller states.

The 'threat' is often seen to be critical to alliance cohesion. Some alliances clearly cannot survive a decline in the threat, or a sense that the threat is irresistible. However, even with a weak sense of threat, a strong sense of shared values and interests can hold allies together. It is also important to note in this context that threat is as much a political as a military concept, with evidence of antagonism as important as the capability to act upon it.

Cohesion also varies according to the consequences of aggregation. It is perfectly possible for the aggregate strength to be far less than the sum of the individual parts. A front-line state might be weak and only capable of being defended through immense expenditure of resources by its allies, which in turn may mean that they are unable to defend themselves. In a symmetric alliance, effective aggregation of strength will rely either on a direct transfer of one state's resources to another's defensive effort or in a synergy between the two efforts (i.e. by opening up a second front); in an asymmetric alliance, resources must be allocated by the strong to the weak. This might soon lose its attraction to the strong if their strength is being dissipated as a result.

The extent to which this is so will only become known for sure in wartime. The limitations of military balances as predictors of a war's outcome are well known. Strains are very likely to develop in any peacetime alliance should war begin or seem imminent, as political and military leaders are forced to question how much they are prepared to jeopardize the national position in order to provide relief for allies which may only be temporary. In a peacetime alliance, however, all the advantages flow in the direction of encouraging confidence in aggregate strength. In these circumstances, a sudden awareness of an immediate threat can undermine cohesion, in that it will push to the fore a series of incipient, difficult questions concerning the capacity of the allies to engage in coalition warfare.

We can thus identify an almost effortless extended deterrence, in which a strong power with a keen concern for the security of the weaker members within an asymmetric alliance can produce a formidable military strength without putting itself at great risk. However, it may still be possible to hold together the alliance if these conditions are not met, so long as there is a positive basis to the alliance, and so long as the immediate threat is not so acute that the full logic of coalition warfare has to be addressed in earnest.

It might be the case that both alliance formation (and, for that matter, disintegration) depend on an acute sense of threat, for only then will states take on new commitments and dependencies. At such times the credibility of the aggregate military response is critical. The argument of this section has been that sustaining the alliance thereafter depends not so much on an acute sense of threat (though whether it can cope with a complete *absence* of such a threat is an interesting question), or the actual quality of the aggregate military capability, as on a positive sense of cohesion based on shared values and interests.

The instruments of deterrence

Alliances have in the past been forged as much by resounding declarations – perhaps backed by consultations between political and military leaders, and possibly promises of an expeditionary force from the participating countries – as by long-term peacetime deployments of one or more states' forces on the territory of another. Hosting garrisons of foreign troops involved risks – for both parties – if they remained while fundamental political relationships changed, and suggested that the host was being reduced to the status of a protectorate.

The toleration of overseas bases in the post-war era was made necessary at first because of their stabilizing influence in what was understood to be a highly unstable situation. The Atlantic Alliance was not initially assumed to depend critically on such basing; it was only as a direct military threat from the East came to be taken seriously that major force commitments were made. Without American – and British – involvement at an early stage there was little chance that Western Europe could resist a determined Soviet push.

What began as a short-term expedient turned into a long-term commitment. The forces began to establish permanence because there was never a good strategic case for their removal and the political case for their retention grew. Strategically, a future war promised little time to prepare and send an expeditionary force, especially if it had to cross the Atlantic. There might be arguments over how many troops were necessary, the appropriate equipment and the most sensible doctrine, but there was little doubt that a serious barrier had to be created to a Warsaw Pact offensive on the Central Front. Given the shape of West Germany, this barrier had to be as close to the border as possible if the country was to be protected rather than cast in the role of a battlefield. The requirement for forward deployment impinged on all allies, and not just the US.

By carrying the main burden of deterrence, nuclear weapons made it possible to avoid continual fine tuning of conventional force levels to match the political tension level. The apparently permanent shift from a state of crisis requiring the constant application of immediate deterrence to the relaxed state readily supported by general deterrence, in part caused by nuclear weapons, in turn made their role easier to sustain.

General deterrence no longer becomes relevant when there is either a loss of a broad political identity, either through internal divisions or the lines of demarcation between the two antagonists becoming blurred at the edges, or else a palpable shift to immediate deterrence.

The problem comes when one contemplates a deterioration in East–West relations such that immediate deterrence will once again be required. Here one comes up against the familiar difficulties of nuclear strategy which over time have created greater trust in conventional forces as the most appropriate instruments for immediate deterrence or for war itself. Conventional forces are in practice largely discussed in this role, rather than in terms of the looser requirements of general

27

deterrence, yet provisions for the forces are still subject to the more relaxed approach made possible by general deterrence. A hint of war can produce exceptional measures – facilities can be requisitioned, military budgets increased along with combat readiness, and so on. These are likely to subside in peacetime, as the requirement shifts again from immediate to general deterrence.

Much strategic debate proceeds as if there is an intense peacetime interaction between the forces of two adversaries in anticipation of war. But to truly prepare for war (rather than simply maintain options and draw up contingency plans) we need to appreciate how it will occur. However, we cannot prepare, because the political context would have to change so significantly for war to move into the realm of possibility. Strategic analysis has handled this problem simply by jumping over it – we move from peace to war without being able to take account at all of any intervening period of tension. We discuss the consequences of deterrence failing in terms of a clash between the two Alliances as currently constituted and with their current (and possibly projected) arsenals. However, one thing we can be sure of is that, if deterrence fails, the political context will bear little resemblance to that of today. Apart from anything else, the alliance system, East and West, would probably be in the process of disarray. This is why we cannot say that extended deterrence can be secured by any particular configuration of military forces.

Furthermore, to the extent that extended deterrence depends as much on alliance cohesion as on military capabilities, certain elements in the force structure gain respect for their contribution to alliance cohesion (often of a contribution of a highly symbolic nature), even when it is not altogether clear that they will be particularly useful in the event of war. Just as the debate over extended deterrence has been institutionalized, so has the significance of the individual elements that make up the forces devoted to this task. Attitudes towards particular weapons reflect assumptions as to the consequences of their actual use. (This is evident, for example, in German views on short-range weapons which are governed by their implications for German territory.)

It is important to be clear that stressing the extent to which deterrence depends on alliance cohesion as much as types of forces is *not* code for minimum deterrence. It means that avoiding chronic political instability within the alliance will take precedence over purely military considerations. This priority is, of course, quite likely to continue even at times closer to immediate deterrence.

The diversity of the NATO Alliance makes this unavoidable. Particular capabilities become politicized in different ways and at different times and then become shaped through the policy-making mechanisms of the Alliance. Some important capabilities never become politicized at all; others which would play a minor role in the event of hostilities become a litmus test of Alliance loyalties and readiness to share risks. The history of Alliance debates by no means suggests that the minimalists always come out on top.

The symbolic debate conducted through force structure and dispositions reflects views as to the risks that each party to the Alliance runs on the others' behalf and the risks that the others are running for them. These views cannot be separated from judgments as to the character of a future conflict. Perhaps all one can say is that in times of immediate deterrence one is more concerned about military efficiency and overall power and less about the principle of risk-sharing (it was not uppermost in British minds in 1940–41). At times of general deterrence these intra-Alliance issues appear more pressing. On the other hand, the sensitivity of this issue is a direct result of concern that in circumstances of immediate deterrence the risks to the United States might render it unwilling to implement the threats made on behalf of its allies.

Conclusion

The reason why extended nuclear deterrence is easier in practice than suggested in theory is that the theory has been too narrowly framed, and the practice has never really faced a severe test. The credibility of nuclear threats is not essential to Alliance cohesion during peacetime conditions of normal East–West antagonism. As there is no reason to expect that the antagonism will become more severe in the near future – if anything it might become less – then there is no need to panic.

However this comforting conclusion is subject to two qualifications. First, under current conditions Alliance cohesion is vulnerable to major shifts in Alliance loyalties and commitments that might occur independently of questions of threat and nuclear credibility. The argument that a more relaxed security environment makes it possible to enjoy the benefits of alliance without worrying too much about the inherent risks can be turned round to make the case that alliance is no longer necessary, so why accept any risks at all. It is important to stress that the continuity of alliance is central to the continuity of the current favourable trends in international relations.

The second qualification concerns the nagging possibility that East–West relations could still take a turn for the worse, which raises the question of how well the current conventional and nuclear force structure of NATO would then cope. There can be no definitive answer to this question. We need not take the ultimate test too seriously, in part because in current international circumstances the prospect of facing a first-use – or second-use – decision is remote but also because of the difficulty of envisaging the circumstances in which we might do so.

In current circumstances, so long as the allies are satisfied with the configuration of forces, then it is satisfactory; in some hypothetical crisis we cannot be sure what will be necessary, precisely because it is so hypothetical. This is, of course, not much help to those policy-makers charged with sustaining extended deterrence. The conclusion that there is no physical solution to the problem of extended deterrence appears to be belied by the persistent arguments within the Alliance on this issue, which tend to revolve around the type and disposition of American forces. Can the Alliance cope with a cut in US troops based in Europe? How will we threaten the same targets that were once threatened by cruise and *Pershing*? Can we do without nuclear artillery? It is not the intention of this Paper to attempt to answer these questions, but it can help in generating criteria for the policy debate.

One of the central difficulties of this whole approach, of course, is that a warm glow of security generated by a conviction that we are in a state of general deterrence can evaporate quickly if this assessment is wholly wrong and there is an urgent need for a strategy of immediate deterrence. If front-line forces decline too far in relation to adversary capabilities, then there is a risk of even a mild crisis being aggravated by a frantic rush to get forces in place. Nonetheless, there is still no reason to take as a central planning assumption that war could break out at any moment.

Ultimately, extended deterrence is essentially about holding together an alliance in times of extreme strain. The most significant test is not therefore faced at the point of complete breakdown in East–West relations but at a point when relations are tending in that direction. That is when war is still distant but just about conceivable. The problem is to maintain options should immediate deterrence become necessary when these options are being developed in the political climate created by years of general deterrence. When the crunch comes, the range of available options will reflect the ebb and flow of alliance politics over many years. In practice what is remarkable is less the extent to which problems of immediate deterrence have been neglected but the extent to which they continue to be addressed.

Both hawks and doves contribute to this state of affairs. This is less surprising with the hawks, who may well consider the risk of a breakdown in East–West relations still to be quite high and so feel a need to be prepared. However, the doves encourage this too – through warnings over the degree to which we are caught in an arms race which must inevitably end in war, or anxieties over American behaviour, or even in advocacy of schemes of 'non-provocative defence' which must be judged in terms of how well they could cope with direct aggression.

Should such a situation arise, then one can expect, as we found in the early 1980s, that attention will turn to the quality of conventional forces. However, while defending against conventional threats with conventional forces is more credible than attempting to deter with nuclear forces, this does not let the nuclear powers off the hook. It is still necessary to deter nuclear threats. In addition, the risk of nuclear escalation cannot be eradicated, and it is undesirable that it should be. The underlying dilemma of having to put oneself at nuclear risk on behalf of third parties cannot be avoided. This dilemma confronts the

UK and France as well as the US, and in certain instances European attitudes towards this dilemma might be as critical for Alliance cohesion as American. At a minimum we might say that to extract the full benefit from finding ourselves in a nuclear age we must ensure that our potential adversaries harbour no illusions as to what nuclear war would mean and remain conscious that they cannot escape its horrors. This may require that they be held directly at risk (which suggests long-range and survivable weapons) and are encouraged to be sensitive to the mechanisms by which this risk might be realized.

There is now little possibility that credibility can be restored to the first-use threat. This does not create a case for a no-first-use promise. To be definite either way is impossible, given the unpredictability of war; existential deterrence depends on this unpredictability, and so the decline of the first-use threat is not fatal for the theory so long as the possibility that nuclear weapons will be used during the course of a war retains credibility. Deterrence in these terms is strengthened to the extent that the USSR sees a possibility that they will be used against its territory and not confined to short-range use.

But the possibility of nuclear use involves tolerating the prospect of a weakening of command-and-control arrangements during the course of a war. The logical tension between existential deterrence and the drive to eliminate the possibility of accidental or inadvertent use is quite manageable so long as it concentrates on tightening command-and-control procedures but more problematic if it focuses on the location of weapons.

There is a case for pulling nuclear weapons back from front-line forces (i.e., to put more stress on stand-off missiles than on *Lance* modernization). However, once one starts to move them back from the territory of allies, then the action involved has ceased to be a prudent measure to prevent unauthorized nuclear use and constitutes a redefinition of security commitments. Extended deterrence has worked through reinforcing a sense of vital interest, by ensuring that the US cannot avoid the consequences should war break out over Allied territory.

Notes

[1] Robert Osgood, *The Nuclear Dilemma in American Strategic Thought* (Boulder, CO: Westview Press, 1988), p. 41.
[2] Patrick Morgan, *Deterrence: A Conceptual Analysis* (Beverly Hills, CA: Sage Publications, 1977).
[3] Typified by Robert Jervis, Richard Ned Lebow, Janice Gross Stein, *Psychology and Deterrence* (Baltimore, MD: Johns Hopkins UP, 1985).
[4] McGeorge Bundy, 'The Bishops and the Bomb', *The New York Review*, 16 June 1983. For a discussion, see Lawrence Freedman, 'I Exist: Therefore I Deter?', *International Security*, Summer 1988.
[5] For an elegant statement of this view, see Philip Bobbit, *Democracy and Deterrence: The History and Future of Nuclear Strategy* (London: Macmillan, 1988).

The Logic of Strategy and the Upkeep of Extended Deterrence

DR EDWARD N. LUTTWAK

Introduction
Just as the tacit premise of US economic policies of recent years is the transcendental immunity of American prosperity to all forms of public and private profligacy, the tacit premise of West European security policies is the certainty of peace.

By a species of strategic *apartheid*, the persistence of war in Africa, Asia and Latin America is deemed the curse of more backward races. In Europe, *bien-pensant* opinion agrees, there can be no war, indeed the very thought of it is bizarre. As a recently retired Chief-of-Staff of the army of one NATO country put it: 'In Europe war has become absurd on a human plane, I mean classic war on a large scale, with divisions moving, bombardments and so on . . .'.[1]

For those who hold the view that the European security equation must always yield the result *Peace*, it only remains to manipulate the variables accordingly.

The institutionalization of optimism
If an observer points out that one NATO national corps is stationed too far from its intended war positions to cope even with the canonical version of a surprise attack,[2] while another is simply too weak in men and machines to put up a respectable defence of its assigned frontage, and yet a third is deployed in a manner that can only facilitate its admission to POW camps after its flanks have been turned, NATO military men answer that everything depends on the counter-attack with theatre nuclear weapons anyway, so that all such petty defects of the non-nuclear defence hardly matter. If, on the other hand, an eminent former US Secretary of State, experienced in the ways of American politics, flatly declares that American consent for the nuclear counter-attack at the theatre level is a fantasy, and a resort to intercontinental nuclear warfare for Europe's sake even more so,[3] diplomats and politicians in NATO countries deplore the indiscretion and go on to stress the solidity of the non-nuclear defence, before insisting on the continued credibility of nuclear deterrence at every level. Thus those who are charged with military responsibilities concede military shortcomings but trust in the political realm, while those who have political

responsibilities trust in the soundness of military preparations, as well as in deterrence – an interesting reversal of roles.

The analytical case for the soundness of NATO non-nuclear military preparations now forms a large literature of its own that has considerable currency in academic circles.[4] It rests on a great many convenient assumptions,[5] which exclude *inter alia* the blockage of transatlantic reinforcements by commonplace forms of interdiction, and such non-measurables as the paralysing effects of surprise, and above all the dislocating effects of exactly those forms of in-depth attack that the presumptive adversary has chosen to emphasize in his own military preparations.

While the budgetary implications of such optimism are not welcomed in NATO circles, the current generation of nuclear-habituated officers virtually accepts its conclusions, at least *sotto voce*. Educated throughout their careers under the assumption that if combat becomes serious it will also become nuclear, they unconsciously categorize non-nuclear combat as not serious. Hence every form of military self-indulgence can be tolerated, be it the refusal of some Defence Ministries to purchase even critical and uncostly gap-filling equipment if it can be neither domestically produced nor included in two-way industrial deals, or the refusal of all of them to stock ammunition in the agreed quantities;[6] be it the failure of some NATO armed forces to train their recruits with some semblance of realism, or the failure of all of them to exercise on a scale commensurate with prospective wartime roles, thus perpetuating an entire generation's ignorance of the actualities of large-scale operations, which differ greatly from any straight sum of the smaller-scale actions that are exercised;[7] be it the cognitive dissonance of one key NATO member in regard to the value of fixed anti-tank barriers, or of all NATO air forces in regard to air-base vulnerability.[8]

The rejected solution: guaranteed Soviet restraint
Even if the insufficiency of non-nuclear defences is admitted, the obligatory result of the European security equation, namely *Peace*, can still be assured in one of two ways.

The first is to assume away the threat by noting, very reasonably, that today's reformist Soviet government seems preoccupied by quite other concerns than the planning of an imminent European war. It was equally reasonable to argue of yesterday's lethargic Soviet government that its complacency was hardly consistent with martial ambitions on a heroic scale.[9] And an even stronger case could be made for the improbability of deliberate war before 1964, when Khrushchev could still believe (with GNP data to back him) that the efficiencies of central planning would ensure the Soviet Union's bloodless, ideological victory by example.

More generally, analogies with the pre-1939 Nazi threat that did materialize have always been easily refuted by citing ample evidence of the Russian cultural, and Soviet ideological, propensities for restraint in confronting first-class powers. A quite different analogy, with the decaying Austro-Hungarian empire of many ethnicities and its sudden 1914 breakout from timidity to aggression, is perhaps more plausible but does not seem to have persuaded many.[10] Neither has the argument that Russian cultural restraint derived from a since-remedied historic lack of military/operational confidence, while its ideological counterpart derived from a since-exploded confidence in the bright future of Soviet society.[11]

In spite of its widespread currency in public opinion, the 'Soviet restraint = Peace' version of the European security equation has always been discounted in policy circles. The reason, of course, is that it is precisely NATO's power to resist and retaliate that motivates Soviet restraint, hence reasonable expectations of the latter require adequacy in the former. (And, whatever the need for such an induced restraint may have been in the past, it must be yet greater now when the reformist attempt of the Gorbachevites is violently agitating a political structure that lacks a stabilizing electoral legitimacy, the cohesion of a unitary nation, or even a settled procedure for the peaceful transfer of power.)[12]

The official solution: defence + deterrence and conciliation = peace
Even while it is formally rejected, the 'Soviet restraint = Peace' solution is actually a hidden component of the second and official NATO solution of the European security equation, whereby 'Defence (D1) + Deterrence (D2) as well as Conciliation = Peace', with D2 always held to be large enough to offset any inadequacy in D1.

This confidence in the assured sufficiency of D2, i.e. of extended (nuclear) deterrence, originally derived from the vast superiority of the American nuclear arsenal, in virtually every weapon category and by virtually every criterion of measurement, and from the validation of those capabilities by the manifest readiness of US public opinion to sanction the *ultima ratio* of a nuclear counter-attack against a Soviet invasion of Western Europe, even if totally non-nuclear. When US opinion viewed Moscow as the source of a global and monstrous menace ('godless Communism'), an equally monstrous nuclear response of global effect was proportionate; now that the threat is viewed in classic great-power terms, as geographically and politically constrained, only an equally constrained response is proportionate.

The earlier and abundant sources of deterrent confidence having passed away, continued belief in the sufficiency of D2 actually derives from the tacit assumption that there is not all that much to be deterred anyway; in other words, from a smuggled-in version of the same 'Soviet restraint = Peace' solution that is quite properly rejected officially as invalid in logic and most imprudent in practice.

It is not only hurried politicians electorally bound to optimism, professionally optimistic diplomats, and military men under orders to be optimistic who thus traffic in smuggled goods; so do a great many academic analysts, including the distinguished author of the most rigorously argued case for the continued validity of extended deterrence known to this author, Richard K. Betts of the Brookings Institution.[13] While his otherwise most impressive argument deserves a close and full reading, its conclusions may be summarized as follows: the *residual credibility* of a NATO nuclear counter-attack (even against non-nuclear invasion), even if still declining, will nevertheless remain sufficient to avert a Soviet decision to attack.

Though more sophisticated in full rendition, the Betts argument ultimately rests on the same simple but powerful propositions as the usual 'deterrence by uncertainty' argument (i.e. the actualization of the 'credibility' of a NATO nuclear counter-attack is the Soviet assessment of its consequences multiplied by the Soviet estimate of its risk); and because of the catastrophic gravity of the consequences, *any* risk estimate above zero, suffices to ensure the credibility of NATOs extended deterrence.

What justifies my claim that this argument contains a hidden assumption of Soviet 'restraint' is its *very nature*. Given Soviet counterforce capabilities (including unconventional ones) against theatre as well as intercontinental nuclear forces (capabilities whose actual 'damage-limiting' effect may be variously calculated, including in ways quite optimistic, thus reducing the assessed consequences), and given the argument's own admission that the estimated risk, while greater than zero, is far short of unity, the argument for 'residual but always sufficient' extended deterrence rests on the more or less prudent calculation imputed to the Soviet leaders of the hour. By such prudent calculation, Adolf Hitler should not of course have launched *Barbarossa* in June 1941, and certainly not declared war on the United States in December 1941; still less should the Imperial Japanese government have launched its own attack on Pearl Harbor.

True, the consequences that could be anticipated by Hitler and Japan were not nuclear. But, on the other hand, they did include a fairly large possibility of defeat, an outcome amply catastrophic for the *decision-makers themselves*.[14] Even more true, no Soviet leader has yet exhibited the manic aggressiveness of Hitler, or the counter-rational military optimism of the Japanese military men of 1941. And, given the consequences of (even non-nuclear) defeat, that alone is *the* decisive difference: i.e. Soviet leaders are restrained, hence 'prudent calculation' can reasonably be imputed to them. *Q.E.D.*

In this manner, the assumption of Soviet restraint, though previously rejected as logically invalid and dangerous in practice, is tacitly reintroduced even in the most careful formulation of the 'D1 + D2 = Peace' equation. And so it must be, once the decline of nuclear weapons from their pristine 'absolute weapon' status is admitted.

For that is the ultimate source of the problem, and not the changed NATO–Soviet equilibria in the various nuclear categories, whose assessment is in any case so variable. Even the most pessimistic post-attack estimates still leave the US and NATO with much greater and altogether more flexible surviving nuclear capabilities than were theoretically contained in the unattacked inventories of the 1950s, during the golden age of highly credible extended deterrence. True, nuclear attack on the Soviet Union itself implies the acceptance of retaliation in kind on the United States, making the Alliance into a suicide pact if those extremes are reached. But that, as has been noted *ad nauseam*, has been true for decades, and was certainly deemed true in the mid-1950s, at the very climax of the golden age.[15]

Hence the true cause of the erosion of extended deterrence, is the decline of nuclear weapons *in toto*, within overall military balances as a whole. Only the fact that such a decline has been surprising, and is indeed still contested by some, should be a matter for surprise, given the entire history of warlike devices.

The logic of conflict and nuclear weapons[16]

If there is one manifestation of the paradoxical logic of conflict that has always been widely familiar, it is the parabolic career of military innovations. As soon as we hear of a weapon of novel design that is supposed to achieve dramatic results, we already begin to anticipate its eventual decline towards insignificance (though that ultimate point may never quite be reached).

The process reflects two contradictory impulses. On the one hand, the physical power of the new weapon increases as designs are perfected, production is streamlined to allow mass production, military organizations adjust to accommodate the new device, and valid tactics, operational methods or strategies are evolved for its use. On the other hand, the greater the impact of the novel invention on the former balance of strength, the greater the intensity of adversary reactions, whereby the new weapon is resisted by technical countermeasures, circumvented by new tactics, operational methods or even strategies, and symmetrically opposed by direct emulation.

Protective features may then be added to the new invention, to evade countermeasures, outflank circumvention and outperform prior equivalents already in adversary hands. Then, of course, there will be further countermeasures, more circumvention and the competitive enhancement of competing enemy weapons. The science contained in the new weapon may also evolve, to yield magnified capabilities, setting off a further sequence of adversary responses.

Once the cycles of action and reaction have turned over enough, yesterday's new weapon may be reduced to futility and universally abandoned as technically obsolete or – on the contrary – it may be more powerful than ever in a physical sense and solidly established in the institutional structure of the armed forces; but in either case it will no longer confer its pristine one-sided advantage to the original possessor. Other things being equal, the balance of strength will therefore tend to revert to its original condition, having, as it were, absorbed the impact of the military innovation.

So it was for the bayonet, which initially gave a wholly disproportionate advantage of firepower to its users – because a quota of pikemen were no longer needed in each musketeer regiment to stand before charging cavalry – and which soon gave no advantage at all. And so it has been for every new device of war, for the paradoxical logic of conflict applies in perfect equality both to the humble bayonet and to the most elaborate of weapons. Only the modalities of the decline vary from case to case.

Simple emulation sufficed to nullify the original impact of the bayonet upon the balance of strength and the conduct of wars. There was hardly any scope for technical countermeasures, normally a most important cause of decline (though the survival of lancers among the cavalry may have owed something to that purpose). And there was little need for circumvention: instead of devising new tactics, or new operational methods of war to evade the bayonet's effect, the device was simply acquired by all, to meet the original bayonet-equipped regiments on an equal footing, with every man a musketeer.

But the case is unusual. Significant military inventions are seldom applied so quickly and fully; their span of one-sided advantage is rarely so brief; there is usually much more scope for technical countermeasures, and much greater need for circumvention – tactical, operational, theatre-strategic or even at the level of grand strategy. The fate of the battle tank is rather more typical of the process.

First, the path from invention to operational application was long; the British trench-crossing device of 1915 did not evolve into a German weapon of deep-penetration offensives until twenty years later.[17] Second, the fielding of competent tank units can still today yield a one-sided advantage, because of both technical and economic barriers to emulation. Third, technical countermeasures appeared from the start, and the anti-tank use of ordinary field guns was soon followed by an expanding torrent of specialized weapons; conventional, low-pressure, reducing-calibre and recoilless anti-tank guns, rocket-launchers and later guided missiles, as well as passive countermeasures including demolitions, minefields, ditches and fixed barriers.

Finally, there has been much scope for circumvention: tactically, by acting from terrain unsuitable to tanks; operationally, by 'elastic' defences that deny rigid fronts that can be pierced, or by 'defences in depth' resilient to narrow penetrations; and at the strategic level, by guerrilla and political action that denies any substantive targets. When the one-sided success of tank forces in spearheading deep-penetration offensives altered the total Franco-German balance in 1940, and later the German–Soviet balance until 1942, the reaction so strongly provoked was also exceptionally broad. It included the circumvention of ground combat *in toto* by the bombardment of the German economy, as well as most of the technical countermeasures and lesser forms of circumvention already noted, and of course emulation, with varied British, Soviet and American copies of the *Panzer* division mixed-force concept. Even as armour forces proliferated, the impact of tanks upon overall military balances waned rather than increased: yesterday's new capability was being absorbed by the full range of pre-existing and still newer capabilities.

When nuclear weapons first appeared on the scene in 1945, it seemed to many that the sheer magnitude of their destructive effect would exempt them from the normal cycle of introduction, culmination and decline. That much was implied by Bernard Brodie's term 'absolute weapon', which implied that the fission bomb would monopolize the conduct of serious warfare by the possessing powers.

The strategic air power precedent
By a coincidence destined to be very important, the advent of nuclear weapons had unwittingly been anticipated. Almost two decades had to pass before the tank's operational potential was understood. The fission bomb was a far more revolutionary invention, and yet there was no hiatus between invention and innovation because the 'strategic air power' theorists, Douhet, Mitchell *et al.*, had already worked out an operational and strategic concept for its role in both peace and war.

Their theory held that the air bombardment of enemy war industry could and would displace all other forms of large-scale warfare altogether. It would be decisive long before the sea power contest of supply and blockade could have any perceptible effect, and it would also outpace the attrition of ground warfare. The further claim that air bombardment could win wars even more directly, by terrorizing the enemy's civilian population into demanding immediate peace at any price, was not integral to the theory but nevertheless gained wide credence in the wake of the 1937 bombing of Guernica.

By 1945 it had been learned that the theorists had been greatly mistaken. The technical error was a gross underestimate of the effort required to deliver each ton of bombs, and an equally gross overestimate of the resulting destruction. Only some of the bombers acquired could be operational at any one time; not all operational bombers could reach their objectives; and only some of their bombs would actually hit worthwhile targets. These cumulative shortcomings left a wide gap between theoretical and actual bombardment capacities.

The error of strategy was a classic example of the 'first-move fallacy': the entire sequence from bombardment to surrender had been envisaged in one-sided fashion without anticipating adversary reactions, other than reciprocal bombardment. Apart from the failure to consider air defences – excusable until the advent of radar – the theorists had ignored the ability of civilian economies to circumvent the air attack, by the dispersal of production, damage-control and reconstitution. And the anticipated political effects were also outmanoeuvred. When the brutalities of warfare were translated from remote battle fronts to cities, and from obedient soldiers to civilians at large, the result was militarization, and not the collapse of the will to fight. In lieu of soldiers, civilians were uniformed and disciplined as air-raid wardens, volunteer firemen and auxiliary police; in lieu of trenches there were air-raid shelters; and in lieu of military obedience there was social pressure, propaganda and police control to stop defeatism and actually extract energizing anger from the bombing. In perfect accord with the paradoxical logic of conflict it was mainly the enemy's air-defence effort that earned advantage for the bombing, by diverting production capacity and manpower from offensive purposes.

The arrival of the fission bomb on the scene unexpectedly rehabilitated the air bombardment theory that had just been refuted. Even a few long-range bombers would now be sufficient, because a single bomb could do the work of ten thousand, nullifying the wide gap between inventory and operational capacities. Industrial damage-control and reconstitution, if not yet dispersal, would be defeated; and no amount of propaganda or police control would overcome the terror of radiation for survivors. As for air defences, even the peak attrition rates of World War II, of 10–12%, would be trivial for bombers that had to attack only once to earn their keep. It therefore seemed that, with the fission bomb, air bombardment could finally have that monopoly of warfare that had been claimed so prematurely. Why keep armies if their supplies would be interrupted almost immediately? And why navies if the strongest warship could be sunk even by a near miss? And why bother to sink fleets at all if their operations would be irrelevant in any case?

But the pre-1939 strategic air bombardment theory had also been a theory of peace – to be achieved by 'deterrence', a word already well established in its current meaning. If any city could be devastated in a single raid, as Guernica had been, a balanced threat of reciprocal bombardment should dissuade war outright. Thus the entire notion that weapons which exceed the culminating point of purposeful destruction could best serve to dissuade war rather than fight it was already familiar, because of a mistaken estimate of what non-nuclear bombing could do. With the fission bomb, however, air bombardment could truly become the arbiter of peace, it was thought, as well as the all-purpose instrument of war.

The decline of nuclear weapons begins

Looking back on that first dawn of the nuclear era in our knowledge that the new weapons neither precluded nor monopolized warfare, we can see that once again the paradoxical logic of conflict proved stronger than any weapon, even nuclear weapons. In their case, however, the causes of decline have been unusual, and the process has been slow for such a fast age – and also by no means uninterrupted. Post-1945 technical advances, which greatly exceeded the destructive capacity of the original combination of fission bombs and piston-engined aircraft, even restored the eminence of nuclear weapons in the balance of power for some years.

Countermeasures – usually the most important cause of the decline – have had an exceptionally small role, just as with the bayonet rather than the tank. The large Soviet air-defence effort has made bombers more expensive but has not substantially reduced the damage they could inflict. Equally, Soviet passive defences, extraordinarily elaborate as they are, have not been the cause of the decline of nuclear weapons in the overall East–West balance of power.

As for emulation – the obvious cause of decline – its importance is often exaggerated, obscuring causes actually more decisive. That is shown *inter alia* by what happened between 1945 and September 1949, when only the United States had the bomb[18] – critical years during which the post-war European order was formed, and frozen. The impact of the fission bomb upon the overall balance of power should then have been at its peak, but that is when *circumvention* first emerged, precisely to reduce the effect of the (American) fission bomb upon the US–Soviet balance in Europe. At the time, the salient Soviet goal was to establish subservient regimes over lately conquered Czechoslovakia, Romania, Bulgaria and Hungary, and the Soviet zone in Germany. Had there been no American fission bomb, direct and overt administrative measures could have sufficed; as it was, in oblique recognition of its power, the Soviet Union relied on subversion. Personal duress secretly applied to leaders of the majority parties induced the formation of coalitions. Later, under the same compulsion, the coalitions began to eliminate democratically elected members by outlawing centre-right and then centre parties as fascist, until the remaining non-Communist leaders dissolved their own parties, leaving the local Communist party in sole control. The wall of implicit atomic dissuasion was never challenged by these invisible proceedings, but a tunnel had been dug underneath it, so to speak.

From those beginnings, circumvention was to grow luxuriantly in future decades, as first the Soviet Union and then the United States resorted to every variety of subversion, guerrilla action by intermediaries and outright third-party warfare, so as to pursue all the classical purposes of statecraft without either engaging their own nuclear strength or providing sufficient cause for nuclear retaliation. The monopoly of conflict that nuclear weapons were to have, and their role in the balance of power, were correspondingly diminished. It was obvious, too, that the scope of circumvention was set by inhibitions on the other side that could exist independently of any fears of retaliation. Hence it was the very strength of the new weapon that was its own undoing – for the first time a weapon could be too destructive.

The fission bomb already exceeded the culminating point of military utility by being excessively destructive for use in any conflict that did not affect national survival, quite apart from any fears of retaliation in kind. Hence a role remained for non-nuclear capabilities even in a direct confrontation. The first Berlin crisis of 1948 accordingly became a contest between the Soviet blockade of overland transport and the Anglo-American airlift; while the United States did not simply order the cessation of the blockade, neither did the Soviet Union interrupt the airlift by intercepting transports or occupying the airfields. From that precedent until now the rule-setting role of nuclear weapons endures: to delimit but not pre-empt the role of all other military forces, and to delimit less and less.

When the Soviet Union acquired its own fission bombs, emulation was added to circumvention to further reduce the impact of the new weapon upon the balance of power. With that, the fission bomb's presumptive monopoly of military power was diminished much more seriously, to the extent that the United States found itself engaged in a full-scale conventional war in Korea, with Army, Navy, Marine Corps and (non-nuclear) Air Force all active on a large scale.

The Korean War had not ended when the fusion bomb appeared. Of far greater destructive capacity than the first fission bombs, it exceeded the culminating point of military utility to an even greater extent, making its use in any peripheral conflict even more implausible. This time, moreover, emulation was much more rapid, with the first American test at the end of 1952, and the first Soviet test in 1953. If the factor of emulation had been as important as some appear to believe, a sharp decline in the importance of nuclear weapons within the overall balance of power should have ensued, with both sides symmetrically inhibited and thus constrained to secure all their interests – except immunity from nuclear attack itself – by purely conventional forces on an equal footing.

Instead, in what appears in retrospect as a triumph of statecraft, the United States claimed a very large asymmetrical advantage for itself under the so-called policy of 'Massive Retaliation' enunciated in January 1954. Capitalizing on the defensive stance of the United States and its allies, which placed the onus of starting war on the Soviet Union (or China); and taking full advantage of the apparent readiness of the American public after Korea to accept nuclear use even to defend peripheral interests, the new policy asserted the exemption of the United States from having to compete in those sectors of the overall military balance (notably ground strength) that were deemed comparatively disadvantageous.

To be sure, the United States did not act in strict accordance with the declared policy. The Army, Navy, Marine Corps and (non-nuclear) Air Force were not disbanded in 1954, nor even drastically reduced – but they were increasingly nuclearized, allowing the parsimonious Eisenhower Administration to justify large savings: measured in constant (1985) dollars, the defence budget declined quite dramatically, from just over $300 billion at the peak of the Korean rearmament in fiscal year 1952 (mostly not war expenditures) to $170.7 billion in 1954, with the total remaining below $200 billion until the advent of the Kennedy Administration.[19] Those were the savings of nuclearization, destined to be undone by denuclearization.

The obvious risk that the new policy was mere bluff, rather than the expression of principled determination, and that the bluff could be called; or the opposite risk that it was not a bluff, and that all-out nuclear war might be unleashed in response to merely peripheral attacks; and the scope that the policy allowed for circumvention in any case – all were criticized by academic experts. And discipline did not silence the military critics who deplored the impossibility of purposeful military operations by all-nuclear forces.

But, for all the authority that these off-stage comments were eventually to acquire, Massive Retaliation was certainly successful in its time. The US budgetary savings derived from the policy were, as noted, substantial, and by all accounts European policy elites felt more secure than ever before or since, in spite of the large superiority of Soviet ground forces. In retrospect, we may recognize those years as marking the culminating peak in the importance of nuclear weapons in American strategy and within the overall US–Soviet military balance.

No stronger form of warfare has intervened to deprive nuclear weapons of their primacy in destructive capacity. And neither has their decline been caused directly by Soviet emulation. It is symptomatic that the policy of 'Flexible Response', whereby nuclear weapons were downgraded to provide a higher court of appeal, as it were, was finally imposed on the Alliance at the very time when, by every criterion of measurement, the superiority of US intercontinental nuclear forces over their Soviet counterparts was at its peak in both numbers and quality. If the balance of respective destructive capacities had been determining, 1967 should have witnessed a reaffirmation of Massive Retaliation rather than its final repudiation.

No physical change in American and Soviet nuclear arsenals can explain what happened. Nothing changed, but everything changed, because mentalities and perspectives changed – at least American mentalities and American perspectives. The risk of a prompt escalation to all-out nuclear war in the event of a Soviet offensive, even non-nuclear and perhaps peripheral, which had been at least passively accepted by American public opinion in, say, 1955, was no longer acceptable ten years later – or even five years later, judging by the policies and declarations of the Kennedy Administration. As noted, the perception of the Soviet threat had changed from one that was unlimited in scope and implication to a classical geopolitical conception in which such and such Soviet forces were seen as capable of invading this or that theatre of war, or destroying this or that target. It followed, therefore, that the defence should also be discrete, with a mix of non-nuclear and nuclear means calculated to yield a 'prudent' level of dissuasion, and a 'graduated' response if deterrence failed.

To the members of the new policy elite that understood all that was measurable and little of what was not, the undifferentiated globalism and absolutist simplicity of Massive Retaliation had seemed absurd in combining both vagueness and cataclysmic resolve. The notion that *status quo* powers very much on the defensive have their own prerogatives, including that of fighting a different war from the one thrust upon them; the recognition of war-experienced leaders, notably Eisenhower and virtually all his European counterparts, that even a purely 'conventional' war in Europe could be abundantly catastrophic, so that the Soviet Union could be deterred just as well by a vague threat of nuclear attack; and, above all, the realization that no warfare in Europe between great powers, and hardly any warfare anywhere, can actually be controlled in carefully defined gradations (the 'steps' of the 'escalation ladder') – all these were disregarded.

But it was not errant leaders who truly caused the decline of nuclear weapons in declared American strategy, and therefore in the overall US–Soviet balance of power. Their conduct at each remove merely reflected particular phases in the irreversible attitudinal shift that is the true cause of denuclearization. What leaders said and did at most accelerated a process that official policy did not control. Policy decisions in fact merely registered the stages of denuclearization – sometimes quite belatedly, as in the case of the 1967 Flexible Response strategy for the Alliance, enunciated long after any immediate recourse to nuclear weapons would have been contemplated in the event of a non-nuclear Soviet offensive against Western Europe. In a manner that its advocates should appreciate, the decline of nuclear weapons in American strategy, and therefore within the overall military balance, can even be illustrated numerically:

Department of Defense Total Obligational Authority by Program ($m current)[20]

| Fiscal Year | Combat Forces | | % | Comments |
	'Strategic' (1)	'Gen. Purpose' (2)	(1:2)	
1950	2,468	5,093	48	Embryonic nuclear period
1955	6,990	13,321	52	Lingering Korea effect
1957	11,182	12,995	86	Nuclear peak year
1960	10,297	12,799	80	Denuclearization begins
1970	6,928	27,651	25	Full Vietnam effect
1980	10,992	52,307	21	Denuclearization advances
1984	26,053	100,493	26	Renuclearization under way
1985	27,682	120,584	22	Denuclearization resumes
1987	21,100	114,900	18	" "

This table does not of course measure the effect of nuclear weapons, but it does indicate the level of confidence successively accorded to them, and their decline from 'absolute' status.

The receding boundaries of extended deterrence
As the denuclearization drift has continued, the unreality of the extended deterrence offered by the United States for other countries, with its implied readiness to start nuclear warfare in response to non-nuclear attack, has gradually been exposed, much as high ground is revealed by receding waters. Because perceptions and objective change are one in this case, it is hard to say with confidence just how matters stand at any one time, but we do see the repudiated past in perfect clarity.

Thirty years ago, the Quemoy and Matsu islands off the Chinese coast – one quite small, the other insignificant – were to be held by nuclear counter-attacks against (non-nuclear) Chinese artillery barrages, under joint US/Republic of China defence plans. Today the notion that the United States was ostensibly ready to use nuclear weapons to defend Quemoy and Matsu seems completely absurd, but it was not so at the time for the officers and officials involved, who would nowadays smile in disbelief at their own thoughts and actions of those days. Similarly, it now seems clear that the denuclearization drift has progressed far enough to rule out the use of nuclear weapons for the defence of South Korea against a (non-nuclear) invasion from the North. That was still a highly realistic option during the 1960s, given the balance of forces – even a prompt necessity in case of an all-out invasion. But nuclear use would hardly be contemplated now, even though the United States remains committed to the defence of Korea, and even though it would be difficult indeed both to defeat a surprise invasion and also shield the Seoul area from damage without the use of nuclear weapons.

According to known plans, Japan is still to be defended by nuclear weapons if non-nuclear defences fail. Such public discourse as takes place mostly addresses the eventuality of American nuclear retaliation for prior Soviet nuclear attack, but that is hardly the salient threat, given the vulnerability of at least Hokkaido to non-nuclear invasion from nearby Soviet territory. Even if one considers American mass-opinion attitudes towards Japan at the time of writing as merely transitory, it is hard to believe that an American President would authorize nuclear attacks against Soviet bases and military forces in response to a non-nuclear invasion; if he did, he might find himself the subject of exceptionally rapid impeachment proceedings.

As we take note of the more or less blatant unacceptability of nuclear use against non-nuclear attack in one setting after another, only the nuclear-aided protection of the Alliance in Western Europe retains enough plausibility to justify debate.

It is impossible to determine how far the continuing drift has progressed, but the trend is clear enough and is best revealed by the size and quality of the non-nuclear forces that the various Alliance members see fit to maintain. In the early 1950s the various frontages in northern Norway, Italy and eastern Anatolia, as well as the 'central front' in Germany from the Baltic to the Austrian border, were guarded only by scattered units, mostly lightly armed, that formed long, thin, notional lines – a very poor defence against concentrated armoured offensives but quite suitable to trigger the nuclear bombardment of the Soviet Union. The very fragility of the 1950s defences added to the credibility of Massive Retaliation, for there was no interposed choice, no conventionally-secured opportunity for controversial deliberations. In the decades since then, NATO units have grown into formations, and their greatly enhanced armament belies the stability of divisional counts; tactical deployments have also become more realistic, and the logistic capacity for sustained combat has increased most of all, and it increases still.

That the growth of non-nuclear forces is the most accurate measure of denuclearization is obvious enough; but this growth also *promotes* denuclearization. Officially it is said that, on the contrary, improved non-nuclear defences promote the credibility of extended deterrence, by raising the visibility, so to speak, of the (non-nuclear) armed clash. But stronger non-nuclear defences also secure the political arena in which the imminent possibility of nuclear use must become the only subject of contention. While non-nuclear defences defend, newspapers can be published, radio and TV can function and parliaments can assemble, all to submit the nuclear-use decision to scrutiny much less rarified than at present. Once the question is asked, can there be any doubt as to the answer, whether in the United States or anywhere in Europe?

Only an attitudinal reversal that must be judged most improbable can now prevent the eventual emergence of Europe's 'post-nuclear' era as I have called it, in which peace will have to be secured as it was always secured before – if imperfectly – by non-nuclear forces and diplomatic conciliation, with nuclear weapons finally confined to a purely reciprocal dissuasion role.

Conclusion: What is to be done
The study of strategy is not a disinterested pursuit, and the uncovering of trends does not imply their passive acceptance. The unprecedented European peace of recent decades is too precious to be recklessly gambled on fragile theories of non-nuclear adequacy, inherent Soviet restraint, inevitable Soviet decline, or on the 'strategical apartheid' thesis whereby Europeans – including all possible Soviet rulers – are simply too civilized to wage war once more. Until expelled by the monstrous destructive power of nuclear weapons, war found its most congenial habitat precisely in the centres of European civilization. If the nuclear monster is increasingly diminished and driven out, war will look in from its exile, to await its chance once more, ready as always to mock all theories of its impossibility.

Certainly it is only the continued presumption of peace, derived from nuclear weapons whose continued European role is by no means assured, that allows us to view the spectacular collapse of regime authority in Eastern Europe, and the novel unpredictability of Soviet politics, with our present equanimity.

While the erosion of extended deterrence must be soberly recognized, it should also be resisted. This requires, first of all, that Alliance governments stop promoting denuclearization in their political discourse. Of late, it has been the leadership of the United States itself that has depicted nuclear weapons as the problem, and their reduction as the solution, in a perverted transposition of the historical reality that war is the problem, and nuclear weapons are the solution. If the reckless delegitimization of nuclear weapons is not repudiated by the new Washington administration, the consequences must be serious.

That, however, is only a necessary condition. The sufficient condition is a reaffirmed Alliance consensus on the continued role of nuclear weapons in its security. The time has come for a Harmel II, in order to first explore and then define an agreed and comprehensive approach to nuclear-weapon modernization, conventional force reductions, and nuclear arms control. Given the confusion that persists in the wake of the INF Treaty, it would be imprudent to attempt nuclear-weapon modernization without prior consensus-building *à la* Harmel I.

Any new nuclear weapons, whether in the form of a *Lance* upgrade or some other configuration, can serve to maintain the currency of NATO's nuclear capabilities, thereby countering at least the physical constituents of denuclearization. But it is obviously preferable, for political reasons as well, to field nuclear forces that can have purposeful military uses. In that regard, it is worth considering weapons of sufficient range and precision to attack *military* headquarters, and specifically the fortified Soviet/Warsaw Pact command centres for theatre, 'front' and 'army' echelons, as well as for frontal aviation, fleets, and certain more specialized forces. No intent of nuclear decapitation is thereby implied, for central Soviet headquarters are further removed and would require weapons of greater range.

Militarily, a counter-C^3 approach offers the advantages of multiple synergisms: first, Soviet commands induced to evacuate fixed facilities would lose the use of land lines, thereby becoming more vulnerable to the electronic and hard-kill disruption of their radio communications; second, the more Soviet C^3 is thus degraded, the clumsier and/or more rigid will be the allocation of reinforcements, reducing the great strength of the Soviet army, which is precisely its vast potential for opportunistic reinforcement (the factor that overcomes at the operational level the tactical rigidity of individual Soviet formations); and third, the more Soviet operational flexibility is degraded, the greater the results that can be expected from FOFA-type or classic air interdiction, both behind the battlefield and in greater depth, thereby validating costly capabilities whose actual operational value is now in doubt.

As important perhaps is the greater political acceptability of weapons specifically designed to target frontal headquarters, rather than more of the innocent, in or out of uniform. If occupied at all in the event, fortified command posts would be occupied by at least some actually responsible for the operational command of the forces of aggression.

It would be premature to add more details to a suggestion that should follow and not precede a Harmel II exercise. But, whatever their exact form, a new force of nuclear weapons represents the only alternative to a process of physical denuclearization whose dangers must not be underestimated. Nuclear-habituated as we are, we have continued to take for granted the fruit of the tree even as we recklessly saw away at the trunk. Whatever the long-term trends may be, the tree that yields peace is worth protecting for as long as possible.

Notes

[1] Personal communication. That officer was unimpressed by the rejoinder that the outbreak of war absolutely requires a pre-pre-war period, in which war is deemed too absurd to warrant either adequate military preparations or earnest diplomatic conciliation, thus allowing the drift to continue to the pre-war period, when preparations provoke, and appeasement incites.
[2] Which itself assumes a longer warning than competent political/operational deception could allow, and excludes a variety of counter-deployment disruptive actions of the sort much employed in recent wars (e.g., Egypt's insertion of helicopter-borne commandos on the Rafah–Kantara axis on the night of 6 October 1973).
[3] Henry A. Kissinger, oft-quoted but still worth quoting: 'our European allies should not keep asking us to multiply strategic assurances that we cannot possibly mean, or, if we do mean, we should not want to execute because, if we [do] execute [them], we risk the destruction of civilization. . . . There is no point in complaining about declining American will, or criticizing this or that American Administration, for we are facing an objective crisis. . . . I ask any of you around this conference table: if you were Secretary of State or [National] Security Adviser, what would you recommend to the President of the United States to do in such circumstances? How would he improve his relative military position [by authorizing the use of theatre nuclear forces]?' From 'The Future of NATO' in Kenneth A. Myers (ed.), *NATO: The Next Thirty Years – the changing political, economic and military setting* (Boulder CO: Westview Press for the Center for Strategic and International Studies, Washington DC, 1980).
[4] The writings of its leading American exponents are serialized in the Cambridge, MA, journal *International Security*.
[5] As noted, most recently, by Elliot A. Cohen in 'Towards Better Net Assessment: Rethinking the European Conventional Balance', *International Security*, vol. 13, no. 1 (Summer 1988), pp. 50ff.
[6] There is a sound strategic argument against stocks so large that they undercut the credibility of the nuclear counter-attack; but there is no strategic justification for unequal stocks for forces meant to fight side by side, and still less for the deceptive conflation of both outdated and modern ordnance in NATO declared stocks (as, e.g., in the case of APDS and APFSDS 105mm tank rounds).
[7] Thus a recent journal article (which denies the Warsaw Pact's superiority in tanks) is prefaced thus: 'Alongside the giant 60-tonne German, British and American war machines, Russian tanks look positively tiny. In addition, NATO tanks have sophisticated thermal imaging and fire-direction systems. One Leo[pard II] can take care of several of theirs, says a German tank officer, and the Americans grin self-assuredly.' S.

Thielbeer, *Frankfurter Allgemeine Zeitung*, 23 June 1987, p. 5, quoted in Malcolm Chalmers and Lutz Unterseher, 'Is there a Tank Gap?: Comparing NATO and Warsaw Pact Tank Fleets', *International Security*, vol. 13, no. 1 (Summer 1988), p. 5.)
Thus officers who have never exercised on a realistic scale, confuse tactical-level 'exchange rates' with the outcome of operational-level encounters between multitudes of tanks, wherein one-unit technical advantages may count for little. (Cf. German World War II *Tigers* versus 'tiny' T-34s, or 'tinier' M-4 *Shermans*.)
[8] *Salty Demo*, a two-week simulation held at US Air Force Base, Spangdahlem, in the autumn of 1985, showed that 'even a fairly moderate Soviet attack could reduce our ability to generate sorties. The degradation was especially severe in the first critical week.' (Tidal McCoy (Assistant Secretary for the Air Force) in *Armed Forces Journal*, September 1987, p. 54). McCoy, organizer of *Salty Demo* and of subsequent remedies, deserves great credit, but the overall vulnerability of US and non-US air bases in the AFCENT region is still so high, even against the postulated threat, that NATO's overall reliance on tactical air power is itself a major vulnerability (for the same reason the dutiful air balance computations of Joshua M. Epstein, Barry R. Posen *et al.* are invalidated, since they exclude a pre-emptive attack on NATO air bases, the logical Soviet move, which happens to be prescribed by Soviet doctrine; Cohen, (*op. cit.* in note 5), p. 67).
[9] The invasion of Afghanistan is not a counter-argument but rather added proof of a feckless complacency.
[10] Edward N. Luttwak, *Grand Strategy of the Soviet Union* (New York: St Martin's Press, 1983) contains a version of that analogy.
[11] *Ibid.*, where both arguments are explained in full.
[12] The Politburo voted for Mikhail Gorbachev's elevation and might vote to remove him, but there are no fixed modalities for any potentially Politburo-overruling summons of the Central Committee or larger CPSU assemblies.
[13] In 'Compound Deterrence vs. No-First Use: What's Wrong and What's Right', *Orbis*, Winter 1985, pp. 697ff.
[14] Even excluding the not necessarily inconsequential concomitant of mandatory death by suicide.
[15] By 1956 Soviet nuclear bombardment of all USAF bomber bases was a respectably calculated threat, implying *a fortiori* less demanding counter-city capabilities; A.J. Wohlstetter, F.S. Hoffman and H.S. Rowen, *Protecting the US Power to Strike Back in the 1950s and 1960s* (Santa Monica, CA: RAND Corporation, September 1956 [classified circulation date]).
[16] For a broader exposition, see Luttwak, *Strategy: the Logic of War and Peace* (Cambridge, MA: Harvard UP, 1987).
[17] Guderian's first *Panzer* division was formed in 1935.
[18] Unlike future money, military power is anticipated rather than discounted; in September 1949 the Soviet Union detonated a nuclear device but still lacked an effective means of delivery, yet it was immediately promoted to the rank of an 'atomic' power.
[19] Office of the Assistant Secretary of Defense (Comptroller) *National Defense Budget Estimates for FY 1985* (Washington DC: DoD), March 1984), Table 6-3, p. 80.
[20] Office of the Assistant Secretary of Defense (Comptroller) *National Defense Budget Estimates for FY 1986* (Washington DC: DoD, processed, March 1985), Table 6-4, p. 68; FY 1986, 1987 from *Air Force Magazine*, May 1988 (Almanac) p. 85.

The East-West Military Balance: Assessing Change

SIMON LUNN

Introduction

Although the military balance between East and West embraces a wide set of relationships, this Paper will concentrate on one aspect of that balance: the conventional situation in Europe. The reason for this relatively narrow focus is obvious. In recent years the precise nature of the relationship between the conventional forces of NATO and those of the Warsaw Pact has become the subject of intense public interest and discussion. A renewed burst of enthusiasm by the Alliance in support of stronger conventional forces has converged with the prospects of new arms-control negotiations on conventional forces in Europe. Both developments focus attention on the question of the current balance. Whether establishing the requirements for force improvements or setting the objectives for arms control, and hopefully doing both in parallel, it is important to understand the existing relationship.

Traditionally, of course, there has been little doubt about the state of the East-West balance. The perception that Warsaw Pact forces enjoy considerable superiority over those of NATO has been a predominant theme throughout the history of the Alliance. It has been a major determinant in the evolution of Alliance strategy and its reliance on nuclear weapons, and has loomed large in all subsequent debates on the potential for change to that strategy. True, from time to time individuals have raised their heads above the parapet to question the orthodoxy of Warsaw Pact conventional superiority, normally to suggest that things are not as dire as officially presented, occasionally to challenge the assumption in its entirety. However, for a variety of reasons these views have had little effect on the overall perception. Now, however, the recent interest in conventional forces has spawned a host of ever more detailed and sophisticated studies, some reinforcing the traditional perception, others challenging it, and many taking fellow analysts to task for getting it wrong or missing the point. While the comment in one such paper that the debate is becoming 'a shoot-out in the battle of the bean counts'[1] may be slightly overdrawn, nevertheless the imminence of new negotiations on conventional forces, and the distinct possibility that the Soviet Union will shortly make available its own data, will ensure that the question of the conventional balance will remain at the top of the Alliance security agenda.

This Paper will examine how our perceptions of the NATO-Warsaw Pact ground force balance have evolved, what factors have been influential in shaping these perceptions, and what implications can be drawn for the current debate and for the task that confronts the Alliance in its search for a more stable and secure conventional environment. It will, of necessity, concentrate on the public presentation and discussion of this issue, correlating wherever possible the public perception with the expression of official views.

To start with, however, it is necessary to review the methodology that underpins assessments of the relative strengths of NATO and the Warsaw Pact. In this respect it is important to remember that such force assessments are developed within different contexts and for different purposes. Firstly, force assessments provide the basis for operational analysis and force planning, and consequently the identification of the improvements required to maintain the credibility of NATO strategy. Secondly, they provide the basis for the development of arms-control proposals and the evaluation of measures designed to achieve greater security and stability. Thirdly, they are needed to inform public opinion of the prevailing situation, and in particular to support official policies and positions concerning both modernization and arms control. It is evident that, although force planning and arms control cover much the same ground in their approach to force assessments, they pose different requirements, and hence their conclusions can be correspondingly different. As will be apparent from the discussions on methodology, this dichotomy between force planning and arms control is significant for the public presentation of data, but, more importantly, it is symptomatic of a more basic problem concerning the roles of modernization and arms control respectively in the elaboration of Alliance security requirements.

The conventional balance in the making
Assessments of the balance are derived from two basic approaches. The first involves comparing the numbers of forces that would be available to either side; the second involves looking beyond the numbers to see how they would perform in combat. However, both suffer a number of problems and limitations, understanding of which is crucial to any study on the conventional balance.

The various stages involved in measuring and comparing the numbers of forces are reasonably obvious. The first step is the development of counting rules. In effect counting rules are common understandings and definitions concerning the area, the types of forces and the timeframe under consideration. They are absolutely fundamental to any relative assessment, because unless the same counting rules are applied consistently to both sides there can be no true comparability. The development, application and explanation of common counting rules is obviously central to the development of Alliance agreed data. It is also essential to understanding the many different force comparisons that now exist, whether produced by national authorities, institutes or individuals. The second step is to assemble the data on Alliance and Warsaw Pact forces, ensuring, to the maximum degree possible, comparability in the forces measured – a process that would appear to be relatively simple in theory, but which is somewhat more complicated in practice. The final stage involves the presentation of the assembled data for public consumption. This involves choice as to which elements to display, and also what level of commentary to provide to explain how the numbers were arrived at.

The major obstacle to any comparison of the East–West military balance concerns the unwillingness of the Warsaw Pact to make available information on its forces comparable to the information available on Western forces in official and unofficial publications. Recent improvements in Soviet openness, as displayed in confidence-building inspections and in the almost grudging release of snippets of information on their forces, are welcome lights on a hitherto shrouded horizon, but the situation remains unsatisfactory. Of course, a substantial amount of information on the organization and training of Warsaw Pact forces can be gleaned from the persistent perusal of Soviet military literature, and on aspects of its weaponry from technical journals and third-country sales. But the fact is that for hard numbers in the overall picture we lack direct evidence. To determine the levels of Warsaw Pact forces we must rely on a series of snapshots gleaned from a variety of sources, ranging from the obvious 'national technical means' and 'humint' (human source intelligence) to others hidden in the mists of intelligence, and also on a methodology which, in terms of the accuracy of the final product, leaves much to be desired. We possess a substantial, but frequently fragmented, amount of hard information on Warsaw Pact forces which is used to extrapolate their totality through reasoned judgment and interpretation. Counting and assessing Warsaw Pact forces is far from a precise science.

Jonathan Dean, a former US Ambassador to the Mutual and Balanced Force Reduction (MBFR) talks, has described the limitations of this process as follows:

> Western estimates of Warsaw Pact forces are therefore for the most part purloined information that remains fragmentary and has to be pieced together in the traditional intelligence mosaic, often through assuming that other units of a similar type are of the same strength or equipment level as a known unit on which specific information is available.[2]

Hence, despite continuous improvements in both intelligence sources and analytical techniques, there are inevitably grey areas and levels of uncertainty in our assessments of Warsaw Pact strengths. As General Galvin recently commented:

> It is difficult to calculate with certainty the number of different units the Pact has, the number and type of weapon systems those units have, and the number of personnel assigned to those units.[3]

Common sense suggests that there are some aspects of Warsaw Pact forces about which we have considerable knowledge, and therefore a high degree of confidence in our assessments, and that there are other areas where our knowledge is less and our confidence correspondingly lower. Common sense again would suggest that major items of equipment in relatively close areas, such as tanks in Eastern Europe, would be in the first category; and that smaller items of equipment in more distant areas, for example man-portable anti-tank weapons in the interior of the Soviet Union, would be in the second.

A traditional area of uncertainty central to these assessments concerns the degree of differentiation among Soviet and East European divisions in their peacetime manning and equipment levels, and consequently their readiness and availability. Clearly, judgments of these aspects have a critical bearing on our assessments of how many Warsaw Pact forces would be available, in what time-frame and with what sort of equipment. This issue has been the subject of considerable discussion in the open literature, and a number of commentators have noted how Western estimates of these criteria have changed over time.[4] As will be seen later, changing assessments of the status of Warsaw Pact divisions have been central to the evolution of our perception of the balance.

It is obvious that our estimates of Warsaw Pact forces vary in the degree of confidence we have in them. How serious are these uncertainties? In presenting the totality of Warsaw Pact combat potential that eventually could be brought to bear against the West they are not significant. However, they are significant in other ways:

- They permit a wide range of assumptions concerning the mobilization, availability and readiness of Warsaw Pact forces – critical determinants in any NATO–Warsaw Pact conflict scenario;
- They are of consequence for arms-control negotiations because of the need for accuracy: it can be argued that a concentration on residual levels removes the need to agree current levels, but the requirement for accurate numbers will remain, if only for presentational purposes;
- They have internal political significance for the production of Alliance agreed data, in the sense that they provide fertile ground for disagreement among nations concerning exact numbers. In this respect it should be remembered that, while the US has a monopoly with its 'eyes in the skies', several nations have a particular 'window' on the forces of the Warsaw Pact (for example, the Federal Republic on the German Democratic Republic; Norway on the Leningrad Military District; Italy on Hungary; Turkey on Bulgaria and the Trans-Caucasus Military District, etc.) and, further, that NATO HQ is a co-ordinator rather than a producer of intelligence. All these factors can make agreement or compromise on final numbers a difficult process;
- Knowledge of Warsaw Pact forces obviously has a direct influence on the development of common counting rules, as there is little point in establishing a definition which data produced by the intelligence community cannot match;

- In terms of public presentation, these uncertainties should mean a greater degree of caution and circumspection over the use of assessments than is sometimes the case, particularly in the public debate. They suggest that concentration on those areas where confidence is highest is not only the most prudent but, for credibility of presentation, also the most sensible course;
- Finally, it is also important to note that uncertainty works both ways. Western assessments could as easily be too low as too high, as was demonstrated during the exchange of information for the INF Treaty.

The second set of problems in developing force comparisons involves ensuring that the common understandings and counting rules for the assessment are consistent, and that like is being compared with like. Underneath any comparison there is a set of assumptions concerning 'the where', 'the what' and 'the when' of the measurement. It is impossible to make any sense of an assessment unless these are clearly understood.

In terms of the geographic area, is it a global assessment or just forces in Europe? If the focus is on Europe, are external reinforcements included? (Yes, for force planning; no, for arms control.) Are France and Spain included? (No, for force planning; yes, for arms control.) Is there an accepted definition, Atlantic to the Urals? How do we determine the Central Region? How do we account for Soviet Military Districts? And so on.

In terms of the forces to be included in any assessment, are we looking at only those actually assigned to NATO or at all forces, including those under national command? Again, force planning focuses on one aspect, arms control on another. If we are looking at manpower, are we including all men in uniform, irrespective of function? Are we distinguishing ground, air, air defence and paramilitary forces? Are we separating administrative from combat-related forces and, if so, on what definition? What about reserve forces? In this latter case our knowledge of Warsaw Pact reserve forces, which is imprecise to say the least, and the great variety of reserve systems within the Alliance make the evolution of a formula that would permit direct comparability extremely difficult.

In terms of the equipment to be measured, it is important to be able to identify specific types of equipment that represent key categories of combat power. However, the multi-role nature of some of these systems (for example, armoured fighting vehicles and helicopters), the rapidity of technological change and even sometimes operational deployment can defy the elaboration of a common definition. A loose definition catches all types but loses the desired degree of specificity; a focused definition frequently cannot cope with the number of variants – for example, the problem of producing an adequate definition for the many types of Armoured Infantry Fighting Vehicle (AIFV).

It is also important to have a clear distinction between equipment in units and that in storage, but again this is easier said than done. For Alliance forces it is relatively straightforward to classify equipment with combat units as 'active', but not so easy to categorize other equipment that is outside combat units and is used for replacement or maintenance purposes. This definitional problem explains why the United Kingdom White Paper for 1988 puts the number of NATO tanks in the Central Region at 8,100, whereas *The Military Balance 1988–1989* reports 12,700 for the same area. In the case of the Warsaw Pact, it is important to remember that Pact equipment is identified through its association with units, irrespective of their readiness status. Knowledge of Warsaw Pact equipment outside units or in stores, however, is very hazy. Moreover, doctrinal differences between the two Alliances – NATO sustains and the Warsaw Pact replaces its units in combat – diminish the utility of the in-units/storage distinctions.

Having arrived at common definitions of men and equipment, the problem then is to find units of account that will express most effectively how these assets would combine as combat formations. Divisions and brigades are most commonly used for this purpose, as traditionally they have been seen as the smallest units capable of being self-supporting and of acting independently on the battlefield. Yet the long-recognized differences in size, organization and doctrine both within and between the Alliances, and periodic organizational changes, mean that for the purposes of force comparisons these units of account are of little use. However, they continue to feature in force assessments and presentations because some form of organizational unit of account is essential, because their use in public presentations is well established and because knowledge of the organization of Warsaw Pact forces is an area in which the Alliance enjoys high confidence.

Finally it is very difficult to reflect the varying degrees of readiness and availability of these units. Units on both sides differ substantially in their manning and equipment levels and in the preparation and level of training of their mobilizable forces. Assessments of the availability of Warsaw Pact forces, expressed in terms of mobilization time and location, and of their readiness (the time needed to reach the required level of training) is a question of judgment rather than mathematical certainty. By contrast, even though we can allocate relatively accurate availability and readiness status to Alliance forces, the question of *when* they would mobilize lies in the uncertain world of political decision-making and is beyond certain prediction. As for comparability, how does one rate the mobilization effectiveness of the West German *Bundeswehr* or the Dutch RIM (Rechtstreeks Instromend Mobilisabel) system both reputed to be extremely efficient) against what we know of Warsaw Pact mobilization potential and practice (not a great deal, and what is known not very impressive)?

Yet assumptions about the availability and readiness of units are critical, because they determine not only the static numbers which are assumed to be in place today, but also the more dynamic calculations of what forces would be brought to bear in a particular time-frame. It is because these assumptions are so variable and often arbitrary that many force comparisons tend to show the total potential that could be available irrespective of scenario or time-frame, a presentation frequently described as the worst case.

In fact, assumptions on availability and readiness in addition to the overall totals are implicit in every assessment, whether static or dynamic. The change in the counting rules used made between the 1982 *NATO-Warsaw Pact Force Comparisons* brochure and the 1984 edition[5] demonstrates this point. The 1982 version, the first publication by NATO of agreed data, presented the divisional count in the whole of Europe as 173 Warsaw Pact divisions facing NATO's 84. This represented the total potential available to either side for an unspecified time-frame and included units of very different levels of readiness and areas of deployment. It was decided to improve the 1984 edition by introducing a greater degree of comparability with respect to the availability and readiness of the respective forces. A new definition of forces assessed to be 'in place and rapidly deployable' was introduced. According to this counting rule the Warsaw Pact had 115 divisions and NATO 88.

One press comment which epitomizes the problem of public presentation was that NATO had reduced the Warsaw Pact threat by 58 divisions 'without a shot being fired'.[6] This reaction ignored the point that the 1984 presentation merely showed the military potential in relation to a different time-frame from that used in the 1982 edition, and hence did not include in this category many of the lower-readiness Soviet divisions.

The 1984 publication also demonstrated the problems of reaching definitions that satisfy the national security interests and perspectives of all NATO members. An agreed definition for 'in place rapidly deployable' forces proved difficult to achieve, and, in the end, Alliance politics necessitated the inclusion of all Warsaw Pact forces, irrespective of their readiness status, in any region contiguous to the Alliance.

By contrast, individual analysts are free to make their own assumptions of what forces would be available and when. Consequently, estimates in the public literature of what constitutes 'in place/ready' forces vary considerably. For example, Jonathan Dean, in an eminently reasonable analysis, suggests that the total number of Warsaw Pact divisions potentially available in this category in Central Europe is 56. However, he then assesses that this number overestimates the readiness of some units and further reduces to 33 the number available for what he terms a blitz attack on the Central Front.[7]

Not surprisingly, other analysts using different assumptions get different results. In this context it is worth remembering that all analysts, whether working on the 'inside' or the 'outside', are dependent for their information about Warsaw Pact forces on the same body of data and the same sources. This is not to say that the intelligence community does not have national and internal differences, or that some individuals are not more privy to sources than others. But the point is that no individual analyst has his own private window on the 'real' numbers. Different views are the result of individual interpretation, judgment and presentation, not some form of divine insight.

Establishing the numbers is only the first stage in assessing the balance. The second is to see what the numbers mean or what they would represent in terms of combat potential. This takes us into the even more complex world of net and dynamic assessments. These involve comparing and equating the relative worth of opposing weapon systems, calculating the most likely scenarios under which each side would go to war, and simulating the likely outcome of conflict. The abundance of literature on this issue obviates the necessity to elaborate any further here on these more sophisticated dynamic assessments. The approaches are many and varied, as are, not surprisingly, the results. It is important only to reinforce the point that any study, no matter how sophisticated, is a prisoner of the assumptions and criteria on which it is based. Many models undoubtedly offer great flexibility in coping with a broad range of variations in input, but their ultimate effectiveness and utility must be limited by the sheer volume of these variables, and above all by those factors that are beyond calculation: the imponderables or 'fog' of warfare. As one analyst has noted:

> So called dynamic analysis – particularly when it involves computer modelling – appears at once more sophisticated and more realistic than mere 'bean counting'. In some respects it may be so. But it has its own perils because of the very seductiveness of simulations, their mathematical elegance and their supposed resemblance to warfare in the real world.[8]

There are, therefore, too many 'ifs' and 'maybes' in such assessments to warrant confidence in their conclusions. This is not to say that such studies cannot make a positive contribution to the process of understanding and defining our security needs. However, when applying their conclusions it is important to maintain a sense of perspective concerning their inherent limitations.

This brief review of the methodology behind our assessments was intended to draw attention to the problems involved in counting and comparing forces. It has focused largely on the question of static assessments because that is where it all begins, and because numbers have always played a major part in public perceptions. Most of the points are known and have been covered in many of the now numerous studies on the balance, but they are all-too-frequently forgotten or overlooked. It cannot be stated too often that any assessment depends absolutely on the counting rules and assumptions that underpin it.

The conventional balance in transition

Perceptions of overwhelming Soviet conventional military power were established in the initial years of the Alliance.[9] In the 1950s NATO statements on the nature of the Soviet ground force threat focused on the total number of Soviet divisions then considered available. It was assessed that NATO faced an overall threat of at least 140 to 175 Soviet divisions at full battle strength (including 25 Soviet divisions in Central Europe fully armed and ready to go), plus 65 to 70 satellite divisions, almost half of these being assessed as effective divisions.[10]

In the political and economic circumstances of the time – European economic recovery, the reluctance to devote more resources for conventional forces and the related reliance on the strategy of Massive Retaliation – this perception of overwhelming Soviet conventional superiority remained effectively unchallenged. During the 1950s the NATO Force Goals adopted at Lisbon were scaled back to a 30-division objective. However, these divisions were to be equipped with tactical nuclear weapons. The prevailing view was that NATO could not match the conventional strength of the Warsaw Pact at reasonable cost, and that nuclear weapons offered a cheap alternative. The comment: 'NATO was thus born with a psychological complex about conventional forces'[11] seems entirely appropriate.

This emphasis on the numbers of divisions was reflected in the first *Military Balance*, published by the IISS in 1959, which stated that the Soviet Union had 175 divisions, of which 75% were stationed in the USSR along its Western border and in Eastern Europe. In East Germany there were 20 divisions, not all up to strength but with 6,000 tanks. In addition, there were 60 satellite divisions in varying degrees of combat readiness. Finally, according to the Institute, it was estimated that: 'The Soviet Union could provide another 125 divisions within 30 days from the date of mobilisation and that she has an overall mobilisation potential of 7 million men.'[12]

Despite the apparently overwhelming nature of the Soviet conventional threat, NATO itself made little reference to the Soviet military threat during this period, in marked contrast to the 1970s and early 1980s. There can be little doubt that this omission owed much to the reassuring, or even distracting, reliance on nuclear weapons under the prevailing Alliance strategy, even though signs of change were on the horizon.

Towards the end of the 1950s the dominant view of overwhelming Soviet conventional superiority gradually came under challenge. As part of the debate on the continuing acceptability of Massive Retaliation, certain individuals began to question whether NATO's position of inferiority was really as bad as the 175 divisions suggested.[13] This point was taken up by analysts in the Pentagon under Robert S. McNamara in order to prepare the ground for his ideas on the need to develop a more flexible strategy. Prompted by the apparent contradiction between the Soviet economic and manpower base and the likely cost of 175 divisions, the Pentagon analysts conducted a cost analysis of the various components of a division – soldiers, equipment, weapons, supplies. Their assessments suggested that only about 80 of the Soviet divisions were combat-ready. The remainder was highly cadred and had major equipment deficiencies. Even the combat-ready divisions were considerably smaller than NATO divisions. Similarly, aircraft had smaller payloads and shorter ranges, and a large portion was optimized for air defence roles. The result of this new methodology was to suggest that NATO's conventional forces were not smaller than those of the Pact.

In short, eliminating paper divisions, using costs and fire power indexes, counts of combat personnel in available divisions and numbers of artillery pieces, trucks, tanks and the like, we ended up with the same conclusion: NATO and the Warsaw Pact had approximate equality on the ground.[14]

Based on these studies McNamara decided that:

The Soviets have superiority in non-nuclear forces in Europe today. But that superiority is by no means overwhelming. Collectively the Alliance has the potential for successful defence against such forces. In manpower alone NATO has more men under arms than the Soviet Union and its European satellites.[15]

In other words, with a little extra effort a credible conventional option in Europe was within reach, if the Europeans wanted it. Thus he urged the Allies to fulfil the 30-division requirement for the Central Region laid down in MC 26/4.

These ideas ran into fierce opposition, both in the US and in Europe, partly for reasons of methodology, but mainly in the context of European reluctance to move to a more flexible strategy. European officials regarded McNamara's ideas as wildly optimistic. German estimates suggested that 50 to 60 NATO divisions would be required for the defence of the Federal Republic alone.[16]

The precise details of this discussion are beyond the scope of this Paper. However, several points emerge from this initial period of examination that are worth noting: firstly, these studies were the first to question seriously the overall Soviet totals and to examine what they meant in terms of actual combat potential; secondly, from this point both the assessment and the perception of the threat became more complex; and, thirdly, both were closely interwoven with political circumstances and objectives. From this time, discussion of the balance at the official and unofficial levels became steadily more detailed and more contentious.

In the late 1960s and 1970s assessments of the scale and seriousness of Warsaw Pact military power were directly related to assumptions concerning the comparative readiness and availability of NATO and Warsaw Pact forces, particularly the large number of Soviet divisions in the Western part of the Soviet Union. The German White Books of the early 1970s consistently attributed a high state of readiness to the approximately 100 Warsaw Pact divisions assessed as available for employment against the Central Region.

Soviet divisions stationed along the USSR's Western glacis are capable of attaining full operational readiness within 24 hours. The same is true of most of the divisions stationed on Soviet territory, whereas the minority of them require from a few days to several weeks to achieve that state.[17]

In a similar vein, the 1969 White Book had commented on the six million trained reservists immediately available for reinforcing the Warsaw Pact as being 'in a position to mobilize and deploy within a short period'. A recent RAND study based on declassified information has provided an interesting example of the criticality of these assumptions to assessments of the balance during this period.[18]

In 1973, at a meeting of NATO defence ministers, Secretary of Defense Schlesinger argued, again within the context of obtaining a stronger conventional posture, that the existing balance was not as bad as traditionally assumed and that, with specific improvements in the right places, NATO could have a robust conventional deterrent. He suggested that the then current assessment of relative strength between NATO and the Warsaw Pact presented an unnecessarily bleak picture, because it failed to distinguish between Warsaw Pact high-readiness and cadre divisions and failed to give NATO sufficient credit for its quantitative and qualitative advantages.[19] On the basis of American studies, he concluded that a situation of rough parity at M-day existed, and even after a period of lengthy mobilization – 30 days for the Warsaw Pact and 23 for NATO – NATO's conventional defences would remain credible.

NATO had already initiated in 1968 a Relative Force Capability Study, partly to offset the continuing reverberations from the US as a result of the McNamara studies, and partly in preparation for the anticipated talks on force reductions (the MBFR negotiations). This study, which was intended to provide a comprehensive review of the balance, engaged in an exhaustive analysis of all elements of the conventional situation, beginning with static numbers and moving on to more dynamic assumptions. While the study was brought to a somewhat abrupt halt in 1974, it provided the basis for NATO's response to the Schlesinger analysis.

NATO officials argued that Schlesinger's calculations for the number of Soviet divisions that would be available for combat were considerably lower, and his estimates of NATO's own forces considerably higher, than Alliance agreed estimates. Moreover, they suggested that the M+23 estimate was used because it represented the most favourable scenario for NATO. In contrast to the Schlesinger assessment, the official NATO agreed position on the threat was an undifferentiated 160 Warsaw Pact divisions.

Again, the point of interest here is not the specifics of the debate but the fact that different assumptions concerning the availability of forces resulted in very different assessments of the balance.

However, while these factors remained important, attention in the early 1970s began to focus on the quality of the respective forces rather than on the numbers available. Public statements on the threat by NATO officials began to draw attention to the extensive modernization programme under way within Warsaw Pact forces:

> The most significant development in Warsaw Pact ground forces is the considerable increase in the combat capability of the Group of Soviet Forces Germany through the formation of additional tank and motorized rifle units and the increase in tank stocks. About 1,500 tanks have been added since 1968.[20]

NATO communiqués, which previously had said relatively little on the quality of Soviet forces, or indeed on the Soviet defence effort in general, began to adopt a more urgent tone.

In June 1970 Defence Ministers: 'noted with concern the continuing growth of the armed forces of the Warsaw Pact'[21] and in December 1976:

> expressed their serious concern at the relentless growth in the strength of Warsaw Pact forces, in which an increasing emphasis is being placed on offensive capabilities . . . which will enable them to carry out sustained offensive operations with little preparation . . . the mobility firepower and logistic support of ground forces have been increased substantially.[22]

The 1975 United Kingdom White Paper noted that: 'over the last 5 years the Soviet Union has improved and increased the capability of its forces to a much greater extent than in any previous 5-year period in peacetime',[23] and the 1977 edition: 'although the number of divisions is unchanged since 1968, their real combat strength in terms of additional tanks, guns, APCs and men has increased by the equivalent of 6 pre-1968 divisions'.[24]

It was these analyses that laid the groundwork for the adoption in 1977–8 of the Long Term Defence Programme as NATO's answer to the increase in Warsaw Pact capabilities.

A more detailed and differentiated treatment of the balance was also reflected in the public domain. In 1968 *The Military Balance* produced its first detailed coverage of the conventional situation in Europe, accompanied by a relatively brief explanatory summary. In subsequent editions the summary became more elaborate and more expansive in explaining the problems of measuring the balance, in providing additional information on issues such as the quality of systems, and in generally putting the raw numbers in a better perspective. Over time, this section on the balance has become the standard reference for all those working in the field without access to classified data (and frequently also for those who have). For an organization as small as the Institute this has been a heavy burden to bear, but most would agree that its track record for objectivity and lack of bias has been exemplary.[25]

The detail contained in the conventional balance section of *The Military Balance* tended to confirm or reflect official statements. Comparison of three of the annual assessments during the 1970s reveal a steady increase in Warsaw Pact numbers (for examples, see Table 1).

Table 1: NATO and Warsaw Pact in the Northern and Central Region
(excluding France but including Soviet forces normally stationed in the western part of the USSR)

	Divisions (equiv)	Ground forces manpower	Tanks (in units)	Tactical aircraft
1969–70:				
NATO	24	600,000	5,250	2,050
Warsaw Pact	65	925,000	12,500	3,795
1974–5:				
NATO	25	620,000	7,000	2,040
Warsaw Pact	70	910,000	20,000	4,350
1978–9:				
NATO	27	626,000	7,000	2,375
Warsaw Pact	70	943,000	21,100	4,055

Among the points consistently stressed in the explanatory commentary was the fact that mobilization would favour the Warsaw Pact, and that the 31 Soviet divisions in Eastern Europe (later reduced to 27) could become 70 to 80 in well under a month. NATO would only reach an advantageous position under a situation of full mobilization. In support of this latter judgment *The Military Balance* consistently showed NATO with more men under arms than the Warsaw Pact.

From 1974, the assessment began to comment in more detail on the question of readiness, suggesting that about a quarter of Soviet divisions in the western part of the Soviet Union are normally Category I. In 1975 this became one third, and there was a considerable reshuffling of the Category II and III divisions. In 1979–80 the number of Warsaw Pact divisions assessed as immediately threatening the Northern and Central Regions was reduced from 70 to 47 by excluding Soviet divisions in the western part of the Soviet Union and the lower-readiness divisions of the East European countries. This reduction was achieved through the adoption of a more focused definition, 'ground forces available without mobilization'. While this explanation was evident from a close reading of the fine print and a comparison with the 1978–9 edition, it was not explicitly clarified in the accompanying notes. This omission reflects a consistent failure among force comparisons to explain when changes in force levels are due to refinements of the counting rules rather than to actual changes in force structure.

Gradually *The Military Balance* began to draw some general conclusions on the trends in the conventional force relationship. In 1974 it commented that: 'The numerical patterns have so far shown a gradual shift in favour of the East; qualitatively NATO has more than held its own'.

In 1975 it noted that: 'the Pact has numerical superiority by some measures, and NATO by others, and there is no fully satisfactory way to compare these asymmetrical advantages . . . the overall balance is such as to make military aggression unattractive . . . [but] the Warsaw Pact appears more content with it than NATO.'

In 1979: 'but in general the pattern is one of a military balance moving steadily against the West.' Thus, in the 1970s both official and public presentations reflected increasing concern at the perceived trends, which were seen to be worsening against NATO. This judgment, however, was based apparently on modernization rates, rather than on simple numerical disparities.

The balance today
During the early 1980s, official views of the conventional situation were, not surprisingly, a continuation of those expressed in the 1970s. But, as the debate has widened, and as more outside observers have joined the fray, this official view has come under challenge and has itself become both more nuanced and more focused. The prevailing view expressed by Alliance officials was one of concern at the continuing modernization of Warsaw Pact forces across the board and the apparently relentless introduction of modern, more capable systems, particularly with the forces deployed forward in Eastern Europe. These improvements were interpreted as greatly enhancing the Warsaw Pact's ability to conduct a surprise attack. Quality was now being harnessed to quantitative advantage in a fashion that suggested an increasingly problematic situation for the Alliance.

In his role as Supreme Allied Commander, Europe, General Rogers consistently stressed that the East had clear military superiority in conventional forces and that the trends were getting worse every year: 'The flywheel on the Soviet military growth machine revolves unabated, resulting in a widening gap between NATO's force capabilities and those of the Warsaw Pact.'[26]

In response to these military concerns over the parlous state of NATO's conventional defences and to the urgings of the United States Congress, the Alliance initiated in 1984 another comprehensive review of its current posture. This review, which involved an examination of major deficiencies and a consequent identification of priorities for the more effective allocation of resources, resulted in the adoption of the Conventional Defence Improvements (CDI) action plan.

One of the principal requirements of this review was an in-depth assessment of the current balance of conventional forces and, in particular, of the precise nature of 'the widening gap'. The results of these studies demonstrated that the widening gap was an elusive concept to pin down; certainly it was difficult to substantiate in numerical terms. Any single comparison with the past depended on the time-frame, area and categories being measured, and in each case it was simply not possible to ensure consistency of measurement between current data and that of the 1970s. Where comparability did exist – for example, with the early 1980s – there was no significant change in the force ratios of the major weapons systems. With regard to the important issue of the number of Warsaw Pact tanks in Eastern Europe, an area where the MBFR negotiations had ensured consistency of measurement, it was evident that, while there had been a substantial increase between 1968 and 1975, the number had since been at a consistently stable (albeit excessively high) level. Similarly, it was found to be extremely difficult to draw definitive conclusions from the qualitative trends. Where comparisons could be made, the picture was mixed, some developments favouring NATO, others the Warsaw Pact. Again, these studies showed the formidable difficulties involved in measuring the quality of particular systems. Comparisons by generation were of little use. Moreover, given the differences in doctrine and style between national armed forces, the selection of essential characteristics and the attribution of values and scores to assess which system was 'better' was of dubious relevance to the real world of combat.

During an Alliance Force Planning Symposium in 1985 it was generally agreed that a more acceptable interpretation of 'the widening gap' was the military judgment that, when all factors were taken into account, the Warsaw Pact's ability to implement its strategy was growing more rapidly than NATO's ability to deny that implementation. The gap was not something that could be measured in simple numbers, but rather was a judgment by the military authorities on the synergistic effect of several trends.

Consistent with this approach, NATO communiques in the last few years have tended to move away from using terms such as 'relentless' and 'build up' to describe Warsaw Pact or Soviet military potential, and to employ more measured and specific language. Rather these communiques have increasingly focused on areas of particular concern: the modernization and 'offensive' orientation of Soviet forces deployed forward in Eastern Europe.

The Military Balance also reflected these trends. In 1981 a new format was introduced with a further change in the counting rules, and the total number of Warsaw Pact divisions in the whole of Europe in peacetime was now shown as 78 – again with no adequate explanation for the change. The accompanying summary concentrated on the quality/quantity relationship and, in this respect, adopted a more pessimistic note than hitherto:

> The numerical balance over the last 20 years has slowly but steadily moved in favour of the East. At the same time the West has largely lost the technological edge which allowed NATO to believe that quality could substitute for numbers. One cannot necessarily conclude from this that NATO would suffer defeat in war, but one could conclude that there has been sufficient danger in the trend to require urgent remedies.

However, the analysis added the following qualification: 'The overall balance continues to be such as to make military aggression a highly risky undertaking.'

This sombre appreciation continued until 1986, when the suggestion that the balance was moving against NATO disappeared. In 1988 the IISS again reviewed the format of its presentation of the conventional balance in Europe in order to conform to the forthcoming arms-control negotiations in the zone from the Atlantic to the Urals. Furthermore, it decided that, because of the complexity of measurements and the significance of the issue (and therefore of the Institute's conclusions), *The Military Balance* would no longer offer a single overall conclusion or assessment of the balance.

The proliferation of differing public assessments has reinforced the Institute's decision to attempt to maintain an effectively neutral position. In the outside debate, lines have been firmly drawn, with some analysts declaring that things are bad and getting worse, while others, looking at different factors, believe that NATO is better off than widely believed. These studies are too numerous to describe here in detail. However, while most provide interesting and new approaches to the problem of the balance, none move us any closer to a definitive conclusion. For, as most of them acknowledge, whatever the originality of the approach or the sophistication of the arguments, their conclusions depend critically on their assumptions. At which point we are back where we started.

The latest development in the debate has been the criticism levelled by two respected analysts, both of whom have worked and published extensively in the field, at the way the conventional balance has been presented and discussed in the public domain. In a typically robust and exhaustive analysis of the conventional balance, Phillip Karber has suggested that much of the public confusion is self-induced, or at least due to the inability of officialdom to explain the facts coherently. He states that within and between Western governments there is widespread agreement on the basics of the conventional balance, but that the description and evaluation of the threat has been conveyed in simplistic portrayals of gross quantitative statistics, rather than in terms of consistently derived and competitively analysed empirical data. The result is the failure of the public to appreciate the true nature of the balance and its implications. To remedy these inadequacies Karber then proceeds to a detailed assessment of the balance, including the dimensions which, in his view, are missing in most public discussions: trends, technology and transition.[27]

For his part, Tony Cordesman takes *The Military Balance* to task, suggesting that in its present form the IISS assessment is 'grossly misleading' and, along with the US Department of Defense publication *Soviet Military Power* is 'useless for either NATO planning or arms control purposes'.[28] The chief problem, according to Cordesman, lies in the Institute's failure to develop comparable rules for counting the forces on both sides, such as those which he claims were developed for MBFR and are now used by Phillip Karber.

It is neither necessary nor appropriate to comment extensively here on either article, except inasmuch as their criticisms demonstrate the problems described in this Paper. In fact, both articles represent part of the problem rather than a solution to it. While there is much in both articles that one can agree with, particularly the call for greater official cohesion and coherence and a higher degree of public understanding, the following points should also be made:

- It is true that official Western assessments are broadly in agreement on overall totals, but that does not eliminate room for different interpretations on the specifics of any presentation, on which aspects should be emphasized and on the significance of factors, such as quality, that are not adequately addressed. The point is that there is no single balance or relationship but many; consequently no single picture can tell the whole story, and each attempt or snapshot will have its own limitations. In short, it is not the messenger who is the problem.
- The fact remains that even Phillip Karber's missing dimensions depend on counting rules and assumptions. Trends depend on the time-frame selected, and their effective comparison upon assurance that the data available from one period is consistent with that from the other, and therefore comparable; assessments of technological advantage require difficult and thoroughly debatable judgments; and comparing potentials for the transition to war again depends on highly questionable assumptions. So again we have come full circle.
- Counting rules are a question of individual or collective judgment. They are not immutable, but change according to improvements in intelligence techniques, technological changes and the prevailing military and political requirements. What was developed and agreed in support of the very early studies on MBFR (the Relative Force Capabilities Study) was never codified and is not necessarily valid or appropriate today. In fact, the IISS method of accounting is closer to current Alliance thinking than several of the points raised in Cordesman's article. But it should be stressed that counting rules are not etched in granite, and they are matters over which honest and reasonable men will differ.

Conclusions

Where then does this leave us in terms of looking at the balance? From the foregoing it is not difficult to arrive at the unremarkable conclusion that assessments of the balance are a function of methodology, presentation and politics. To deal with the last point first, it is clear that political objectives and circumstances have always played a role in the way assessments have been generated, presented and received. Perceptions of our strategic needs and the appropriate weight to be accorded to nuclear and conventional forces, fears of (or preparations for) force reductions, economic constraints, domestic concerns and political bias have all contributed at various times and in varying degrees to the way we have assessed and presented the balance.

Accepting that these political factors are never far from any force comparison, is there a conventional situation out there which we can objectively measure and present with confidence? Beyond all the 'ifs' and 'buts', are there hard indisputable numbers? The answer has to be a qualified Yes. But there is no single presentation which can do justice to the complexity of the situation. Each presentation – whether global or Central Region, manpower or equipment, forces ready today or ready tomorrow – shows a particular dimension and has its own limitations. Each omits as much as it conveys.

However, there are certain aspects of the conventional relationship on which we can and should focus, and which can be stated with a reasonable degree of confidence. For example, it is clear that in the Central Region, and in a relatively short time-frame, the Warsaw Pact has the potential to bring to bear greater numbers of fighting men and key categories of combat power than NATO. The extent and seriousness of these disparities would depend on the time and circumstance of conflict. How they would translate in a combat situation would depend on the imponderables of warfare. However, the size, disposition and orientation of these forces constitute a source of justified concern for the West, particularly when placed within the context of Soviet doctrine.

Obviously, there are other relevant factors to be considered beyond the numbers, just as there are other disparities that merit attention. But it is important to concentrate on those aspects that we consider to be both the most critical for security and stability and also those in respect of which we have the greatest confidence in our assessments. The focus on Warsaw Pact forces in Eastern Europe brings these two requirements together.

The question of focus and balance is particularly important in terms of public presentation. Discussion of the conventional balance is a subject that lends itself to a degree of overstatement which the nature of the subject does not support: a possible development becomes a certainty, an interpretation a fact, and today's assumptions become tomorrow's agreed intelligence. Moreover, while the audience frequently requires simple, clear answers, the complexity of the issue suggests formulations that are frequently imprecise and heavily qualified. Yet a balanced approach is important for several reasons: First, persistently to overstate or exaggerate the problem risks undermining the credibility of the Western position; as A.P. Herbert once wrote, 'the thirteenth chime renders suspect all that went before'. Secondly, to focus on an area which is not immediately significant, or for which the evidence is weak, could distract and even detract from the areas of critical concern – for example, the disparity in tanks is of greater consequence and certainty than the disparity in overall manpower. And, finally, to underestimate or ignore the disparities in the existing relationship will only hinder the eventual achievement of a more secure and stable conventional relationship in Europe.

Thus it is imperative to encourage an open, frank and objective discussion on the nature of the balance – one that searches for more effective ways of assessing and presenting the balance, while acknowledging its inherent complexity. One thing is clear, there is no simple solution, no magic formula waiting round the corner. But that is no reason why we should not collectively look for ways that will inform rather than confuse the public debate. It would also help if the discussion could be conducted unfettered by *hubris*, institutional prejudice, or the pull of the market-place.

The public presentational aspect is not helped by the different role that assessments of the balance perform with respect to arms control and force planning. Both these processes have the same objective of enhanced security and stability, but they approach them from different directions and impose different requirements. In seeking to establish a basis for negotiations, arms control looks at the peacetime balance and assesses all active forces irrespective of their role and status, focuses on individual types of weapons and is concerned with the accuracy of the final numbers. Moreover, it excludes forces not present in, but relevant to, the area under consideration. Force planning is concerned with the operational implications of the existing situation, and therefore with only those forces relevant to planning purposes – for example, those formally committed to the Alliance, irrespective of status or location. It is more concerned with dynamic analysis, with the synergy of combined forces and with force ratios. Obviously there is considerable overlap between the two. Analysis for force planning must start with the static numbers; likewise, arms control must be aware of what lies beyond the static picture, and any proposal must be subject to operational analysis to see its potential consequences for force planning. But, in terms of presenting the balance, the different perspectives can produce confusingly different representations of the same subject.

However, the difficulties imposed on the public presentation of data by the different approaches of arms control and force planning reflect a much deeper, and ultimately more significant, issue: one which permeates much of the current discussion concerning the conventional situation in Europe. This concerns the inherent tension between a strategy and a force planning process that explicitly accept a position of conventional inferiority – as recorded in the time-honoured words 'we do not need to match the Warsaw Pact man for man or weapon for weapon' – and an arms-control approach which inevitably focuses on parity or equality in numbers as an outcome.

This contradiction represents the tip of a doctrinal iceberg and conceals a series of delicate and uneasy compromises on the relationship between deterrence and defence in Alliance strategy, on the respective roles of nuclear and conventional forces within that strategy, and on whether the ultimate objective is to render aggression unattractive or to win a war. The issue that lies at the centre of these arguments is, of course, that of stability – what it is, how we define it and how we achieve it.[29] This issue is beyond the scope of this Paper, except to the degree that it reflects the basic dilemma of developing meaningful assessments of the conventional balance that can be utilized equally effectively by arms control and force planning.

It is well recognized that stability is a complex concept in which the actual numbers available to either side constitute only a single element. There are many other factors that must be taken into account, such as the location, status and quality of the opposing forces, to name but a few. The problem is that, while some of these factors are tangible, others are variable, and many simply unquantifiable. From an operational perspective, it follows that any proposal that seeks to improve stability must take account of these factors and will inevitably reflect this inherent complexity. Yet it is doubtful that the arms-control process can accommodate this complexity, either from the perspective of developing an agreed position that is negotiable or, perhaps more important, that is capable of commanding public understanding and support (what is commonly known as the T-shirt test). The very nature of the arms-control process lends itself to the development of simple, concrete and easily comprehensible proposals. Although less than optimal from the military perspective, such proposals will be politically sustainable, within the context of existing strategy and the prevailing political and economic climate, as enhancing security and stability. What is less certain is whether they will withstand the more testing and exacting examination of the operational analysts.

These practical and theoretical difficulties notwithstanding, it is important to do everything possible to bring the different perspectives of modernization and arms control together. In an ideal world, and all things being equal, force planning and operational analysis would define the baseline of defence requirements upon which an arms-control proposal could be constructed, as for example in the recent study by the RAND Corporation.[30] However, we do not live in an ideal world, and all things are never equal. Moreover, it is no accident that such a baseline has never emerged through the force-planning process, although the Conventional Stability Talks (CST) process has stimulated discussion of NATO's minimum needs. Dynamic operational analysis can be used to demonstrate and evaluate the range of potential consequences from specific proposals. But, because of the uncertainties and variables that underpin these assessments, they cannot be the primary determinant in developing arms-control proposals. Whether we like it or not, our negotiating proposals will owe more to rule-of-thumb calculations of what the political/military market can bear than to the fine-tuning of operational analysis. As Robert Blackwill, another former US Ambassador to MBFR, has commented:

Any sensible Western arms control proposal should proceed logically from judgements about the relative military capabilities of the two sides. But since so much of this determination is based on factors which are subjective and difficult to quantify, proposals are likely to continue to rely for their conceptual basis on simple 'bean counting', crude as that approach undoubtedly is.[31]

Or, to put it another way, in developing Western arms-control proposals there is little to be gained by going much 'beyond the bean count'.

Thus, whatever the level and nature of the future debate, numbers will continue to provide the baseline, particularly in the context of arms control. Which brings us back to the initial problem of getting that baseline right. For the Alliance this objective is well in hand. Work under way for the last two years to create an Alliance-agreed data-base for use in the forthcoming CST negotiations in Vienna is now close to completion.[32] Two tasks remain. The first is for the Alliance to make this data available to the public in a way that is clear and comprehensible – which means explaining, to the greatest degree possible, how the numbers have been generated.

The second task is to engage the Warsaw Pact on the general question of data. While an actual data exchange at this juncture would appear premature and possibly even counter-productive, initial discussions on ground rules and understandings could be a useful beginning. The Soviet Union has professed several times to be ready and willing for a data exchange; however, the information released publicly thus far hardly substantiates this position.[33] It is to be hoped that in the not too distant future the Soviet leadership will feel able to provide a comprehensive and detailed assessment in support of its views of conventional balance. Then the fun will really begin.

Notes

[1] Phillip Karber and A. Grant Whitley, 'Time Technology and the Stability of the Conventional Balance in Central Europe', Paper delivered to conference in Brussels, 25 April 1988, p. 5.
[2] Jonathan Dean, *Watershed in Europe* (Lexington MA: Lexington Books, 1987), p. 44.
[3] General John Galvin, *NATO's Sixteen Nations*, April/May 1988, p. 18.
[4] David M. Shilling, 'Europe's Conventional Defence', *Survival*, vol. 30, no. 2, March/April 1988. Shilling notes that 'one of the most important changes [in our intelligence on the Warsaw Pact] has been a more realistic estimate of the readiness of Soviet ground forces' (p. 126). See also Stephen J. Flanagan and Andrew Hamilton, 'Arms Control and Stability in Europe: Reductions are Not Enough', *Survival*, vol. 30, no. 5, September/October 1988, p. 450, and Dean (*op. cit.* in note 2). A recent Soviet publication has provided the following information on the readiness of Warsaw Pact divisions: 'Category I divisions (about one quarter of the total number) are in full combat readiness in peacetime; Category II divisions (also about one quarter of the total number) require one month to become combat ready: Category III divisions (over a half of the total number) require several months to become combat ready. In order to use the divisions of the latter two categories (they represent a considerable majority)

it would be necessary to mobilize about two million people.' *Disarmament and Security, 1987 Yearbook* (Moscow: Novosti Press Agency Publishing House, 1988), pp. 371-2.
By contrast *Soviet Military Power* states that 'ready divisions constitute about 40 per cent of Soviet forces... and can begin combat operations after a brief period of mobilization and preparation. The not ready cadre divisions can be assembled in about a week and the mobilization divisions require even more time. An extensive period may be conducted before these units are committed to offensive action, although Soviet doctrine allows for their commitment to combat almost immediately after mobilization.' *Soviet Military Power: An Assessment of the Threat 1988* (Washington DC: USGPO, 1988), p. 89.
[5] *NATO and the Warsaw Pact: Force Comparisons* 1982 and 1984 (Brussels: NATO Information Service), p. 8.
[6] *The Guardian*, 1 July 1984, quoted in Lutz Unterseher, *Conventional Land Forces for Central Europe, A Military Threat Assessment*, Peace Research Report No. 15 (Bradford: Bradford School of Peace Studies, March 1987), p. 16.
[7] Dean (*op. cit.* in note 2), p. 56.
[8] Eliot A. Cohen, 'Toward Better Net Assessment; Rethinking the European Conventional Balance', *International Security*, Summer 1988, vol 13, no 1, p. 65.
[9] For a thorough discussion of early perceptions of Soviet forces, see Matthew A. Evangelista, 'Stalin's Postwar Army Reappraisal', *International Security*, Winter 1982/83. See also Thomas W. Wolfe, *Soviet Power and Europe, 1945-1970* (Baltimore MD: Johns Hopkins UP, 1970).
[10] 'What we really have then is 175 Soviet divisions, roughly 65 to 70 satellite divisions, almost half of the latter being effective divisions' (testimony of General Gruenther, Chief of Staff, SHAPE to Senate Foreign Relations Committee, 1954). Evangelista notes that not until the mid-1950s did US intelligence begin to indicate in their classified reports that not all Soviet divisions were at full strength (*ibid.* p. 3).
[11] Alain C. Enthoven and K. Wayne Smith, *How Much is Enough? Shaping the Defense Program, 1961-1969* (London: Harper and Row, 1971), p. 119.
[12] *The Soviet Union and the NATO Powers: The Military Balance* (London: Institute for Strategic Studies, 1959), p. 2.
[13] 'We have accustomed ourselves to saying... that we are hopelessly outnumbered by the Communist bloc. This statement as a generalization is simply not true... The fact is that the Free World can defend itself solely by the force of conventional weapons if its leaders are prepared to pay the price.' Maxwell D. Taylor, *The Uncertain Trumpet* (London: Stevens and Sons, 1959), p. 138.
[14] Enthoven and Smith (*op. cit.* in note 11), p. 140.
[15] Speech by Robert McNamara, University of Michigan, 18 June 1962. Report of the General Affairs Committee of the Western European Union, Paris, March 1963, p. 46.
[16] For a detailed discussion of the political background to the development of Flexible Response, see Jane E. Stromseth, *The Origins of Flexible Response* (London: Macmillan Press, 1988); and David Schwartz, *NATO's Nuclear Dilemma* (Washington DC: Brookings Institution, 1984).
[17] White Paper 1971/1972, *The Security of the Federal Republic of Germany and the Development of the Armed Forces* (Press and Information Office of the German Federal Government, 1971), p. 16.
[18] Jorg Baldauf, *How Big is the Threat to Europe: Transatlantic Debates over the Balance of Forces* (Santa Monica CA: RAND Corporation, P-7372, October 1987).
[19] In his presentation to NATO, Schlesinger argued that: 'The Pact Order of Battle contains 58 stationed and indigenous divisions in the Central Region west of the USSR (not including Hungary), compared with only 29⅓ divisions and 12 brigades in a comparable area on the NATO side (including Denmark and France). However, Pact divisions, even at full strength, are substantially smaller than their NATO counterparts. When we count men in combat and support units instead of adding up divisions, we find that the Pact deploys about 730,000

men, while NATO fields around 685,000 in a comparable area'. 'Depending upon what is being counted, the Pact has numerical superiority in tanks (14,500 to 6,100) and total aircraft (2,800 to 2,750), but NATO possesses important quantitative and qualitative advantages in tank destroyers, anti-tank weapons, armored personnel carriers, trucks, logistic support, and – most important of all – modern offensive aircraft' (Baldauf, *op. cit.* in note 18, pp. 14, 15).

[20] Unclassified briefing on Warsaw Pact Military Progress by Rear Admiral Poser, International Military Staff, NATO, 25 May 1973.

[21] Defence Planning Committee Communiqué, Brussels, 11 June 1970, *NATO Final Communiqués 1949–74* (Brussels: NATO Information Service), p. 240.

[22] Defence Planning Committee Communiqué, Brussels, 9–10 December 1976, *NATO Final Communiqués 1975–80* (Brussels: NATO Information Service), p. 56.

[23] *Statement on the Defence Estimates* (London: HMSO, Cmnd. 5796, 1975)

[24] *Statement on the Defence Estimates* (London: HMSO, Cmnd. 6735, 1977).

[25] It goes without saying that in the preparation of *The Military Balance* the Institute relies on the assistance and advice of officialdom in various national and international organizations, particularly to indicate whether estimates are 'in the ball park'. But in the calculation and presentation of its data the IISS has always borne full responsibility.

[26] General Bernard Rogers, *NATO Security: Myths and Realities*, presentation to Duke University, October 1984.

[27] Karber (*op. cit.* in note 1), p. 4

[28] Anthony H. Cordesman, 'Fatal Flaws in Presenting the NATO/Warsaw Pact Balance', *Armed Forces Journal*, July 1988.

[29] For an interesting and insightful discussion of the concept of stability, see Stephen D. Biddle, 'The European Conventional Balance', in *Survival*, March/April 1988.

[30] James A. Thomson and Nanette C. Gantz, *Conventional Arms Control Revisited: Objectives in the New Phase* (Santa Monica CA: RAND Corporation, N-2697-AF, December 1987).

[31] Robert D. Blackwill, 'Conceptual Problems of Conventional Arms Control', *International Security*, Spring 1988, vol. 12, no. 4, p. 42.

[32] This work is within the context of the High Level Task Force 'Red Blue Team Exercise'. It has involved a comprehensive assessment of Warsaw Pact and Alliance conventional ground and air forces in the 'Atlantic to the Urals' area, including the identification of key categories, the development of counting rules adequate for assessing the forces of both sides in a consistent fashion, the reconciliation of national intelligence estimates of Pact forces and a thorough reassessment of Alliance forces.

[33] See the numbers provided in *Disarmament and Security, 1987 Yearbook* (*op. cit.* in note 4), p. 378.

An Unfavourable Situation: NATO and the Conventional Balance

DR JAMES A. THOMSON*

Introduction
The view, long and widely held, that NATO conventional military forces are inferior to Warsaw Pact forces is one of the most important factors shaping post-war history. It influenced the size and nature of the American military commitment to Europe. It is at the heart of the 'extended deterrence' strategy, in which the US commitment to use nuclear weapons in the defence of Europe offsets the Warsaw Pact's perceived conventional superiority. The notion of Western inferiority runs through much of today's public debate on security policy – the INF Treaty, the future of nuclear and conventional arms control, US and Allied defence programmes, the burden-sharing debate, and so forth. These debates have spawned a new round of discussions on the nature of the conventional military balance in Europe and will affect US and Western policies.

The term 'balance' conjures up the image of a scale, with the Warsaw Pact's military power placed on one side and NATO's on the other. This reflects the normal 'bean count' approach to the military balance: the total number of tanks, artillery, combat aircraft, etc., is the surrogate for military power. The image of the scale conveys a deeper meaning, however: if the Warsaw Pact were militarily superior or the balance were unfavourable to NATO, then NATO would, by implication, lose a military conflict in Central Europe fought with purely conventional weapons. That perception is the one that has shaped the broader Western policy debate.

Because the ultimate use of balance assessments is to understand what sort of defence and arms-control policies are needed to repair the balance, the scale image (and the bean count approach) is not especially useful: it would produce policies aimed at equality in numbers, something the West has not sought. Instead, policies are needed

---

* The author is indebted to many RAND colleagues whose research and ideas have influenced his, especially Paul Davis, Nanette Gantz, Robert Howe, Richard Kugler, Bruce Nardulli and Kenneth Watman. The contents and the views expressed here are not necessarily endorsed by The RAND Corporation or any of its research sponsors. The research was supported in part by RAND and in part by The Ford Foundation. An earlier version of this Paper will appear in Lawrence Freedman (ed.), *Military Power in Europe: Essays in Memory of Jonathan Alford* (London: Macmillan, forthcoming).

that will avoid a NATO defeat in the event of conflict or – in more sophisticated terms – would reduce the likelihood of such defeat and thereby enhance deterrence. That is the approach of this Paper: to assess the military balance in Central Europe in terms of a potential military conflict, and thus provide a basis for the development of policies that would reduce the chances of a defeat.

The term 'defeat' requires some explanation. NATO's strategy of Flexible Response is ambiguous about the objectives it expects its conventional forces to meet. From a maximalist view, it implies that NATO forces ought to provide an unyielding defence, and that any loss of territory would be a defeat. A minimalist view would imply that only an initial defence is needed to give NATO enough time to make the momentous decision to escalate to nuclear war. Clearly, therefore, a judgment of what would constitute defeat in a conventional war depends on one's view of the role and credibility of NATO's nuclear escalation strategy. This Paper does not seek to provide that judgment, but rather to assess the probable outcome of a conflict fought purely with conventional weapons. In this sense, it leans toward the maximalist view for the purpose of the analysis.

The issue must always be approached in terms of probable outcomes. A war in Central Europe would be a massive undertaking. Military operations on a continental scale are shaped by factors too numerous even to begin to list. Some of these factors can be estimated (or guessed at) in advance, but many simply cannot be. Unfortunately, among the latter set are many of the factors that, history suggests, shape war outcomes, such as the quality of military leadership or the national will of the nations at war. In the face of the extreme complexities and the myriad unknowables, it is tempting to say that it is pointless (or hopeless) to attempt to assess potential war outcomes. But this would amount to evasion of a key issue; the perception of a probable NATO defeat will continue to pervade the Western security debate, and defence and arms-control policies will be developed on that basis. Better that the policy debate be informed by analysis rather than conducted in a factual vacuum. But the analysis needs to account for as many factors as can reasonably be included. The best that can be said about such analyses is that they project the probable outcome of conflict, if all other things (e.g. military leadership) are held equal.

Central Europe is not the only place that a war for Europe could be decided. Some analysts argue, on the one hand, that Central Europe cannot be held if the flanks are lost, or, on the other, that the flanks cannot be protected without holding the centre. Rather than focusing on this issue and the underlying strategic choices implied by it, this Paper will concentrate on the likely outcome of a potential battle for the centre of Europe – more precisely the Federal Republic of Germany. The division of Germany is the essential feature of post-war security in Europe. Across the dividing line, East and West confront each other with the largest peacetime concentration of military forces in history. Were Germany to be lost to the West as a result of conflict, the post-war security order would be undone, and NATO – an Alliance whose purpose is to protect that order – would be decisively defeated.

The geography and the forces
From the Baltic Sea to the Austrian border, the eastern frontier of the Federal Republic spans some 650 to 750 kilometres, depending on how one accounts for variations in the border. NATO forces need to be deployed to defend this frontier. If the frontier with Austria must also be defended (to protect against a potential Warsaw Pact invasion up the Danube corridor), the frontier could be as long as 900 km. Of course, the longer the frontier, the more difficult the defence problem, because larger forces must be deployed to protect it. Whether the Soviet Union and its Warsaw Pact allies would violate Austrian neutrality is one of the many unknowables. The military advantages would be substantial, despite Austrian resistance. But there would be political costs, including the potential animus of such other neutrals as Sweden. But some assumptions are necessary. Generally, Western analysts have assumed that Austrian neutrality would not be violated and that NATO would have to defend only the frontier opposite East Germany and Czechoslovakia. That is the assumption made here – an optimistic one from the NATO viewpoint.

This frontier's terrain is varied. The southern region, the area to be defended by NATO's Central Army Group (CENTAG), is fairly hilly, thus potentially channelizing the movement of attacking Warsaw Pact forces and providing traditional advantages to the defence. The hills taper off to the north, where the frontier lies across the north German plain, historically a much-used invasion route. The defensive problem of NATO's Northern Army Group (NORTHAG) is generally viewed as the more difficult. However, the softness of the soil (especially in marshy areas), increasing urbanization and the need for modern armies to exploit the road network limits the scope for large-scale manoeuvre and provides some opportunities for the defence. Nevertheless, there are some 14 invasion corridors across the frontier, requiring NATO to spread its forces, and thus complicating the defensive task.

Germany's strategic depth is shallow compared with the length of its frontier. The Rhine is only 150–200 km from the frontier. Other important military objectives, such as Hamburg and Bremen, are close to the border. The CENTAG region is somewhat deeper, but behind the largely hilly frontier the terrain opens up, facilitating westward movement.

The long frontier and the shallow depth of the Federal Republic have shaped NATO's strategy for defending Germany. Yielding ground to buy time, either for the arrival of reinforcements or for negotiating a favourable settlement, has been ruled out on military grounds: the danger of rapid defeat is too high. It would also be politically infeasible, because maintaining Germany's territorial integrity is critical to its participation in NATO. NATO's strategy of forward defence, therefore, will defend the Federal Republic as far forward as possible.[1]

In brief, NATO plans to establish a heavily defended line in the best available defensive terrain near the frontier. Forward of that line, NATO forces would fight a 'covering force' battle, designed to delay and weaken advancing Warsaw Pact forces before they meet the main NATO resistance in the main defensive zone. The zone would be defended by national corps, four as part of the NORTHAG (Dutch, German, Belgian and British corps), and four as part of CENTAG (two American and two German corps), each assigned a sector along the frontier. The northernmost region of Germany would be defended by the equivalent of a corps formation consisting of German and Danish troops.[2] The essence of this plan – the establishment of a forward defensive line and the layer-cake arrangement of national corps sectors – has often been criticized on military grounds. The linear defence is viewed as too vulnerable to penetration and envelopment. The layer cake invites operations designed to split the defence along the seams created by corps boundaries. But, whatever the validity of these criticisms, the forward defence strategy is a political fact of life and unlikely to be changed. There is, however, considerable scope for altering the tactics used to conduct the defence; doctrinal innovations have been introduced in Allied armies over the years, such as the recent shift of US Army doctrine to the so-called 'AirLand Battle' doctrine.

We are, of course, not privy to Warsaw Pact plans for conducting military operations against NATO in Central Europe. At the political level, Soviet and other Warsaw Pact leaders assert that their strategy is defensive. But the structure of Soviet forces, and their military writings and practices, show that they have been heavily influenced by the lessons of World War II and believe, whatever the political rhetoric, that the best defensive strategy is one based upon large-scale offensive operations. In the Central European context, these operations would seek to establish several main attack axes to push through the NATO defensive line and thus open the way for armoured and mechanized spearheads to move deep into German territory, envelop and destroy NATO forces, and seize key military objectives in the rear, bringing about a decisive defeat as rapidly as possible.[3] In the context of this analysis of a purely conventional war, a decisive military defeat means an outcome in which large portions of West German territory have been overrun.

To conduct its forward defence, NATO would rely initially on existing forces in Central Europe. The most immediately available would be those in West Germany today: the 12 divisions of the *Bundeswehr*, the 10 brigades of the German Territorial Forces (which require large numbers of reservists to bring them to full strength), three British divisions, and four divisions, two brigades and two armoured cavalry regiments from the United States. Small Belgian and Dutch contingents are also present in Germany in peacetime, as the lead elements of their national corps. The remainder of the Belgian and Dutch forces (totalling five divisions) are nearby in their home countries. Three French divisions are in south-west Germany. All told, NATO would have the equivalent of roughly 34 divisions on the ground in Central Europe in peacetime, plus 1,300 combat aircraft.[4] Those forces committed to NATO's defensive line would have to be moved from their peacetime positions to their intended wartime deployment areas, a process that could take several days, because of the need for manpower mobilization and movement over long distances, especially in the case of the Belgian and Dutch forces. If forces not committed to the NATO defensive line, such as the German territorial army and French forces, were made available to defend the central front, they would assume roles as rear security forces and as 'operational reserve' forces to be committed to the battle when needed.

NATO's operational reserves would be increased by deployments from outside the central region. To speed reinforcement, the United States already has in the region sets of equipment for six divisions, called POMCUS (prepositioned overseas materiel configured in unit sets). Soldiers would be flown from the United States and draw this equipment out of storage, so that a total of ten US divisions could be in place fairly quickly, although the call for ten divisions in ten days[5] is probably optimistic. Additional reinforcements – active and reserve US Army units – would be deployed by sea with their equipment. The United Kingdom plans a modest reinforcement of the central front (roughly one division), and seven small divisions in France are potentially available to NATO. Reinforcements, mainly from the United States but also from the United Kingdom, would substantially increase the air forces available for the central region. This air reinforcement could be accomplished in several days and would be a crucial addition to NATO's overall capability.

NATO's 34 divisions in Germany, Belgium and the Netherlands contrast with the Warsaw Pact's 57 in Poland, East Germany and Czechoslovakia. The Soviet units are organized into 'groups of forces': the Northern Group of Forces (NGF) in Poland, the Central Group of Forces (CGF) in Czechoslovakia, and the Group of Soviet Forces in Germany (GSFG) – 26 divisions all told. The East European forces in these three countries contribute another 31.

The Warsaw Pact can draw on Soviet forces deployed in the western USSR as reinforcements for a central battle. It is generally believed that the forces in the westernmost Military Districts – the Baltic, Belorussian and Carpathian – would reinforce the central front as a second 'strategic echelon' for Warsaw Pact operations in this military theatre.[6] Forces from the Kiev Military District could also be committed for this role. A major question revolves around the role of the forces deployed further to the rear, but still west of the Urals. These are generally considered to be the strategic reserves of the Soviet high command, and they could obviously form subsequent strategic echelons and be committed to a war for Germany. Thus, depending upon the allocation of the Kiev Military District and strategic reserves, 40 to 80 Soviet divisions could be available to reinforce the central front. If the USSR decided to attack up the Danube corridor through Austria, this presumably would involve some or all of the six Hungarian and four Soviet divisions based in Hungary.[7] Figure 1 on p. 78 depicts the Soviet Military Districts.[8]

This totalling of forces masks important political assumptions. The potential role of East European forces has been a topic of research and debate in the West for many years.[9] It is clear from the figures cited above that East European forces would contribute a substantial amount to a Warsaw Pact offensive, especially one launched with only the forces present in Central Europe in peacetime. Moreover, because Soviet reinforcements would be deployed to the forward area by rail, and supplies would be moved forward by a combination of road and rail, security of the lines of communication in Eastern Europe would be essential. Hence, Soviet forces would depend heavily on the co-operation of their East European allies in any large-scale offensive against the West.

This co-operation cannot be assured. To a degree, Eastern Europe is under Soviet military occupation. Just as Soviet forces threaten the West with the potential for offensive action, they threaten to impose Soviet will on Eastern Europe through military suppression, should undesirable political trends emerge. Three times since the establishment of the Warsaw Pact, the Soviet Union has used its forces to put down political uprisings. It invaded Hungary in 1956 and Czechoslovakia in 1968. Although it did not actually invade Poland during the height of the unrest there in 1980–81, it came to the brink,[10] and the show of force associated with these invasion preparations certainly affected the course of politics in Poland and the ultimate decision of General Jaruzelski to impose martial law in December 1981. The legacy of bitterness created by four decades of Soviet occupation of Eastern Europe raises the obvious questions of whether East Europeans would fight alongside their Soviet allies and of whether the lines of communications would remain secure. Poland is obviously the biggest problem for the USSR: it makes the largest military contribution of the East European countries, the critical lines of communication run through Poland, and it has the most recent record of political unrest.

Soviet military planners are obviously aware of this problem and have taken steps to deal with it. At the military level, for example, the Warsaw Pact military structure is a thoroughly Soviet organization, with Soviet officers in key command positions throughout.[11] Soviet control extends into the East European armed forces: at the beginning of the 1980s, the USSR 'already controlled virtually everything that was connected to the defense of Poland and the functioning of the Polish armed forces'.[12]

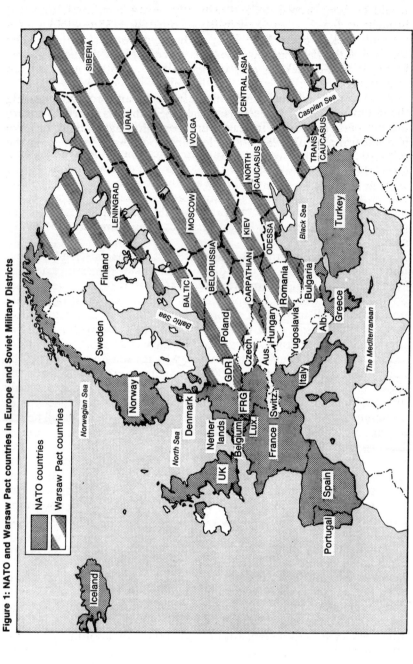

Figure 1: NATO and Warsaw Pact countries in Europe and Soviet Military Districts

The Soviet Union would obviously also seek to ensure popular support in Eastern Europe for any offensive against the West. How this would be done would depend critically on the conditions that had brought on the crisis and possibility of war. The USSR would almost certainly seek to portray the West as the aggressor and claim that the survival of the East European nations was at stake. Outside East Germany, it would seek to play on long-standing latent anti-German sentiment.

What then should be done with East European forces in assessing the military balance? If it seems to the USSR that its efforts to ensure the full participation of its East European allies have failed, or have had uncertain results, the Soviet leaders would have to question the military feasibility of war against the West. East European unreliability would probably deter the Soviet Union from undertaking such an adventure in the first place: this factor is no doubt an important part of the deterrence equation today. By the same token, therefore, a Warsaw Pact offensive against the West, when deterrence has broken down, would almost certainly involve the full participation of East European allies at the outset. However, East European participation could come into question if the offensive bogged down and the possibility of a stalemate or a NATO victory increased.

From the standpoint of a balance assessment designed to help shape Western defence and arms-control policy, the full participation of East European forces ought to be assumed. Whatever steps can be taken to increase Soviet concerns about the reliability of the East European allies obviously enhance deterrence. But the most productive step in this regard would be to create a balance of forces in which the East Europeans were quite dubious about Soviet success. The less they believe Soviet victory is assured, the more likely they will be to hesitate.

The problem of potentially unreliable allies is not unique to the Warsaw Pact. History is full of examples of hesitating allies, even those on good terms before the crisis. Crises are loaded with ambiguity: some signals point towards war and others away. Sovereign nations make independent judgments of their national interest, of the portents of the crisis, and of its probable course. NATO is an alliance of 16 sovereign nations, of which 13 belong to the integrated command structure. In any crisis leading to war, there would certainly be differences among them as to the appropriate course of action. On the crucial question of the decision to prepare military forces for war, it would not be surprising if one or more nations hesitated. In a crisis, Soviet political strategy would certainly be aimed at bringing about a splintering of the Alliance, because of the potential this offers for a Soviet victory without military action.

What should be done about this uncertainty in balance assessments? Since balance assessments are intended to shape defence and arms-control policy, standard assessments must assume that all NATO allies act in concert, as they have committed themselves to do. To assume otherwise would create a fractious political debate within the Alliance (opening the question of which ally or allies are unreliable) and would require compensation for such unreliability, either by building up larger NATO forces or via arms-control negotiations. Neither course seems politically acceptable.

In this regard, however, France poses a special problem. Since 1967, it has not been part of the NATO integrated command structure. French leaders have repeatedly stressed the independent role of France in defence affairs, creating uncertainty as to the potential timing and nature of any French military commitment to the defence of Germany. Another uncertainty surrounds the potential wartime role of French forces, particularly whether they would operate under the NATO command structure if and when France did commit them. In wartime, operations independent of the integrated command structure could be ineffective, especially because French forces are needed as operational reserves for SACEUR, to be committed to the battle at crucial times and locations. Such decisions must be taken by SACEUR and his subordinates. Similarly, the operations of French air forces need to be well co-ordinated with those of NATO forces and would optimally operate directly under a NATO command.

France has recently inched closer to NATO in military affairs. Especially in the last few years, the statements of French leaders have been increasingly forthcoming concerning France's determination to participate in the defence of Germany.[13] These are obviously positive developments, but France's absence from the integrated command structure still leaves troubling uncertainties from a military standpoint.

Table 1: Forces potentially available for conflict in Central Europe

	Divisions		Aircraft	
	NATO	WP	NATO	WP
In Central Europe	34	57	1,300	3,300
Additional forces	6–20	40–80	2,000	700

In summary, Table 1 indicates the raw resources available to the two sides in the event of a conflict in Central Europe. In NATO, the range of uncertainty associated with the reinforcing divisions indicates, on the low side, those US and British forces immediately available for rapid reinforcement and, on the high side, adds further American and French forces. The Warsaw Pact figures reflect the uncertainty about the commitment to a central front battle of the forces in the Kiev Military District and of the strategic reserves of the high command. On both sides, the uncertainties about reinforcements are compounded by the possibility that these forces would be needed in other theatres.

Although divisions are widely understood military entities and are commonly discussed as a measure of military capability, they are actually not particularly useful for that purpose. In the West, especially, divisions come in a range of sizes, with varied organization and weaponry. Analysts seek to overcome this problem by totalling the number of weapons available to the two sides, but such bean counts fail to account for weapons quality. In the early 1970s, the US Department of Defense began using a scoring system that accounted to some extent for quality. This so-called WEI/WUV system assigned scores to individual weapons and summed the scores of all weapons in a military formation to reach a total score. For simplicity, these totals are usually expressed in terms of the score of a US armoured division, which counts as one 'division equivalent (DE)'.[14] With the WEI/WUV system, the total of NATO DE in Central Europe is 27, and those of the Warsaw Pact 40 – a force ratio of about 1.5:1 in favour of the Warsaw Pact. This compares with the actual numbers of 34 and 57 divisions and reflects the fact that, on average, NATO divisions are somewhat stronger than their Warsaw Pact counterparts.

Similar problems exist for air forces, because aircraft have widely varying qualities. A scoring scheme could, in theory, be constructed to account for the contribution of air forces in the close air support mission – providing additional firepower to assist front-line forces. But the principal advantage of aircraft is their ability to concentrate rapidly in specific locations, not their overall firepower *per se*. Moreover, air forces play more roles than close air support – for example, air defence and interdiction strikes behind the front line. Many aircraft, especially on the NATO side, have multi-role capabilities, in that they can be used for ground attack or air defence, depending upon the situation. For these reasons, a simple scoring scheme is not appropriate; the value of air power must be estimated through a simulation (a matter discussed later in this Paper).

The time issue

In addition to the force totals, a crucial determining factor in balance assessments is the time available to the two sides to prepare those forces for combat, which dictates the availability of forces at or near the front line (and therefore available for combat), the readiness of those forces (and thus their effectiveness), and, on the NATO side, the time to prepare defensive positions. Seeking to estimate this time leads to the question of the scenario for war.

In political-military war games it is nearly impossible to get a war started in Central Europe. In the 1950s and 1960s it was fashionable to write scenarios around a crisis in Eastern Europe, which would then spill over into a broader East–West confrontation. Crises outside Europe, in the Middle East or Persian Gulf, have been the object of more recent scenario writing. Any political scenario is easily subject to ridicule. For this reason, most balance assessments simply set this question aside and make fairly simple assumptions about preparation time. For whatever reason, the Warsaw Pact begins to prepare its forces for combat (on mobilization or M-day). After a period of time, NATO detects these preparations, assesses them as preparations for war and begins its own preparations for the defence. At some later point, the Warsaw Pact opens hostilities. For example, in a '10/5' scenario, Warsaw Pact forces prepare for ten days; NATO detects these preparations, and begins its own five days later; five days after that hostilities begin. As discussed later, the choice of specific scenario is one of the most important assumptions of any balance assessment.

The forces of the two sides are at varying levels of readiness in peacetime. Generally, the forces on both sides in the forward areas – in West Germany, East Germany and western Czechoslovakia – are at fairly high levels of readiness; they have their full complement of equipment and of manpower. The equipment is maintained and the soldiers are trained according to standards set by the military authorities for individual small-unit and large-unit training. Even in the forward area, not all NATO and Pact units meet high readiness standards. Many units, even fairly ready ones, require a modest amount of augmentation with mobilized reserve manpower. On the NATO side, others require major mobilization, especially the units of the German Territorial Army and the American Army's Reserve and National Guard units in the United States. Belgian, Dutch and French forces are at intermediate levels of peacetime readiness.

But the readiness issue commonly concerns Soviet and East European forces. Soviet forces are often characterized in three categories: Category I – fully ready; Category II – intermediate levels of readiness, requiring mobilization of up to half the units' manpower complement; and Category III – low-readiness units that require the bulk of their manpower to be mobilized and perhaps also maintenance of their equipment.[15] Soviet units in Eastern Europe are Category I, while those in the western USSR fall mainly into Categories II and III.[16] East European forces vary between all three readiness categories. Thus, the Warsaw Pact will have to mobilize substantial numbers of men to bring its units to a wartime posture.[17] Because these men will not have been recently trained, refresher training will be necessary to improve the training standards of the units in basic soldier skills, as well as in manoeuvring at units level.

Lack of training readiness would obviously affect the combat capability of military units, but analysts have differed over how to account for this problem. Three approaches have been used. In the first, the problem has been ignored: military units move forward as soon as the time needed to mobilize (gather the manpower in garrison) has elapsed (a few days); the units are then considered as fully ready.[18] The second approach allows time, not only to mobilize, but also to bring the units to full training readiness before they can be moved out of garrison. Estimates of the time required for this vary. One estimate uses 30 days for a Category II unit and 60 days for a Category III;[19] another suggests 30 and 130 days.[20] Obviously, lower peacetime readiness units would not figure in the balance assessment for short-preparation-time scenarios under this approach. The third approach, which this author favours, is to degrade the capability of units to account for their lack of training readiness. As time passes and the units train in garrison or in the field, training readiness grows until it reaches a threshold, at which point the unit would be permitted to move forward. If it entered conflict, its capability would be degraded to account for lack of training readiness. This third approach is preferred over the second because it seems foolish to assume that units would be withheld from battle in order to make some marginal gains in training readiness. Better that they fire their weapons at the enemy than at targets.[21]

The readiness categorization schemes have been designed for combat units. Yet the support structure must also be made ready. Training requirements for support units are not as testing as for combat units, but training is still necessary. Moreover, because training needs are not as demanding, support units are often held at lower readiness than combat units, and thus rely to a greater degree on mobilization. This entire issue is often ignored in balance assessments, but it is unclear whether this omission favours NATO or the Warsaw Pact.[22]

The peacetime active support structures of the two sides differ markedly. For example, in Central Europe, Warsaw Pact tanks outnumber NATO's by 2.14:1, and, according to the DE measure discussed earlier, the combat superiority of the Warsaw Pact is 1.6:1. Yet the Warsaw Pact has only a 1.2:1 advantage in active-duty manpower.[23] In peacetime, therefore, NATO has a larger support structure for its combat forces than does the Warsaw Pact. Why? One possible explanation is that this will be changed upon mobilization – the Warsaw Pact is postulated to rely more heavily on mobilization to flesh out its support structure, and to draw heavily on the civilian economy for some aspects of support, such as motor transport. Another possible explanation is that the Pact relies on a lower level of support because of its doctrine. Manoeuvre warfare doctrine, which analysts ascribe to the Warsaw Pact, requires a smaller support structure – 'the more elegant the tactics, the smaller the staffs, the simpler the C^3I and the smaller the logistics tail'.[24] Whether the Warsaw Pact's doctrine is more 'elegant' than NATO's, defensive doctrines seem to require larger support than offensive ones. The attacker can pick the time and place of his offensive and focus its support on the main axes, whereas defenders must be prepared to provide a strong defence over a broad front.[25]

In balance assessments, once combat units have been mobilized and trained to whatever readiness level is deemed necessary by military authorities, they must then be moved forward and positioned for combat. On both sides, those forces near the border would probably move under their own power over the road network to their assigned wartime positions. More distant forces would probably move by rail, because the movement of mechanized forces over distances greater than 100 km is likely to lead to maintenance problems. Soviet forces from the western USSR would presumably move forward by rail, unload, and then move to their wartime positions over roads. On the Western side, POMCUS units would probably also move by a combination of road and rail, once they have obtained their equipment. Forces currently based in the United States, without prepositioned equipment, would of course move by rail to seaports and then by sea to the theatre.

Estimating the time required for these movements on both sides is no easy matter. Factors such as the time it takes to load, move over a crowded road or rail network, unload, and move forward again on roads, must be taken into account. So also must be the requirement for Soviet forces to 'transload' – shift from the wide-gauge Soviet railroad system to the narrower (standard) gauges in Eastern Europe. Always hovering in the background of such estimates is Murphy's Law, which certainly applies to the conduct of large-scale movements.

By most estimates, the Warsaw Pact would be able to move most of its forces into position in one to two weeks.[26] Given the optimistic nature of transportation calculations, it would be wise to err towards the latter figure. Full NATO forces would obviously take longer. Most of the forces in Central Europe could be in position in less than a week, but US POMCUS units and reinforcing divisions from France would take longer, perhaps as much as three weeks. Only after several weeks would forces deployed from the United States by sealift begin to arrive in the theatre.[27]

Time is also especially important to NATO as the defender. In a few days, the combat units and combat engineers could provide hastily prepared defensive positions that would provide added benefits to the defence – forces could be dug in, mines laid, tank traps dug, bridges blown, etc. The longer the units have to prepare their positions, the more strongly they will be entrenched and the more difficult they will be for Warsaw Pact attackers to dislodge. This important advantage to the defence, which of course depends heavily on the war scenario, needs to be considered carefully in analyses of the central front battle.

Methods of assessment

Thus far we have considered the raw military resources available to the two sides, the problem of accounting for the different sizes of units and the quality of their weaponry, and the time issue. These sorts of data are the essential ingredients for an assessment of the conventional balance in Central Europe. But how should these be combined to provide an estimate of the probable outcome of a conflict? More to the point, how should war be replicated to determine the potential outcome given these input data? What is the model of conflict?

Essentially, three broad categories of models have been used. At one extreme is the simple theatre-wide force ratio model. At the other extreme are combat simulations, which seek to model combat in considerable detail. In the middle are simple models that try to account for at least some of the details of war, albeit at an aggregated level. The simplest model employs force build-up curves and theatre force ratios. Figure 2 is an example of build-up curves.[28] On the Warsaw Pact side, the central front is reinforced by forces from the three western Military Districts, plus the Kiev Military District, ultimately making available a total of roughly 80 DE in the central region. The movement of low-readiness forces is delayed until they reach a threshold of 70% training readiness. However, in the figure their combat scores have not been degraded to account for this lack of training readiness.

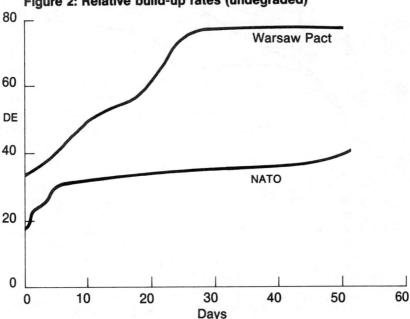

Figure 2: Relative build-up rates (undegraded)

Similar rules have been applied to the NATO build-up curve, which represents a steady dribbling-in of US POMCUS and French units until US sealift begins to arrive towards the end of the time period. Both curves depict a simultaneous start of preparations on both sides.

The effect of the Warsaw Pact readiness issue is depicted in Figure 3. The second curve in this figure is taken from the Pact build-up curve in Figure 2. The third curve degrades the combat capability of the forces to account for their lack of training readiness. The first and fourth curves represent the two extreme approaches to the Pact readiness issue discussed above. The first curve ignores the problem; the fourth curve assumes that Warsaw Pact forces are not moved forward until they have completed their training activities and been brought to full readiness: 30 days for Category II units.

With the simple force ratio model, such curves are used to generate theatre-wide force ratios. Figure 4 on p. 87 demonstrates such force ratios for a 10/5 scenario – ten days of pre-war preparation by the Warsaw Pact and five by NATO. The four curves correspond to the four sets of assumptions in Figure 3.

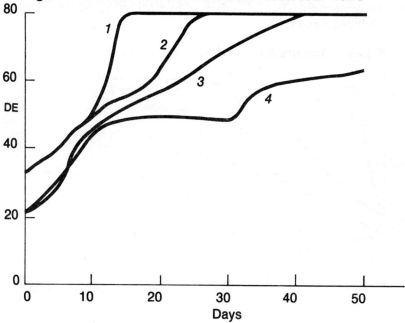

Figure 3: The Warsaw Pact readiness issue: four views

1 Rapid Warsaw Pact build-up
2 Movement of low readiness units delayed until partially ready
3 Same as 2, plus capability degraded in lack of training
4 Movement of low readiness units delayed until fully ready

In a force ratio model, analysts often simply use a threshold to resolve the question of the probable war outcome – force ratios below the threshold would imply reasonable confidence of NATO success. A threshold of 1.5:1 has become practically the standard. This number has been derived from an assumption that an attacker with less than a 1.5:1 theatre-wide force ratio advantage would be unable to generate the local superiorities of 3:1 generally understood as needed for a successful attack in a narrow sector of the front. The origins of all these numbers are murky and dubious.[29]

Of course, none of these force ratios says anything about air power. NATO's air forces are generally conceded to be superior, because of superior aircraft, avionics, munitions and pilot skill. To account for this superiority, the argument is occasionally made that NATO could be comfortable with adverse force ratios in excess of 1.5:1. Figure 4, which is derived from Figure 3 and the NATO build-up curve in Figure 2, indicates that, for a 10/5 scenario, NATO would be disadvantaged in all cases except when lack of Warsaw Pact training readiness prevented the deployment of Category II forces for about 30 days. If NATO could accept 2:1, because of air superiority, then curve 3 would also be comfortable. But 2:1 is derived by adding an arbitrary number to a dubious number.[30]

Figure 4: Theatre force ratios

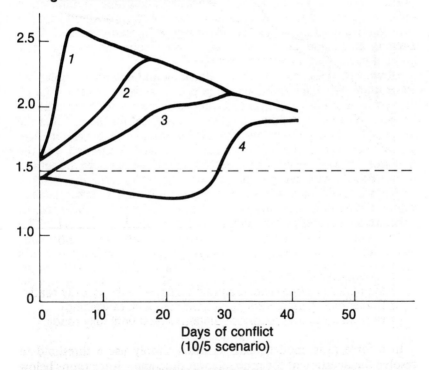

Although, as indicated by Figure 4, the force ratio model is a crude – far too crude – approach to assessing the balance, it does indicate some of the effects that assumptions can have on the balance. Depending on one's view of the readiness issue, the assessment can swing from pessimistic to optimistic. A very-long-warning scenario (not depicted in Figure 4) in which NATO has, for example, two months to prepare, and the USSR does not commit its strategic reserve, would have a positive outcome for NATO because of the arrival of US Army units in Europe by sealift.

Recognizing the fact that the simple force ratio model is far too crude, many analysts, mainly American academics, have published models that account for other important military factors, especially space and attrition rates.[31]

Space, the length of the frontier and force-to-space ratios can come into play in two ways.[32] Defenders are able to provide a stalwart defence if they can create the necessary minimum linear force density, say 25 km per division. Attackers, however, are only able to concentrate their divisions to a finite extent, say 12.5 km per division. This so-called 'shoulder-space' constraint arises because units need to move in march formations and over passable terrain, especially roads. It also can reflect the attacker's need to spread his forces to reduce vulnerability to nuclear attack. If the defender can continue to maintain a sufficient force density, the shoulder-space constraint will prevent the attacker from gaining the 3:1 advantage supposedly needed for a breakthrough, and the defence will remain coherent, even if it is pushed back.

Obviously, the degree to which attacking and defending forces are destroyed would have an important impact on such a calculation. Often these 'attrition rates' have been calculated according to the Lanchester equations.[33] In essence, these laws seek to account for the fact that the superior force can concentrate fire on the inferior one with greater effect than the converse. The inferior force is ultimately destroyed, and the superior one will prevail. The validity of these laws has been the subject of hot debate, with heavy criticism and proposed alternatives.[34]

The academics have also sought to account for other factors, such as advance rates during combat, the advantages of prepared defences, air support, the expanding character of the front as bulges occur, and C³I.

In general, the academics have provided more optimistic assessments of the balance than implied by the widespread perception that NATO is seriously deficient. This optimism results more from the input assumptions – the raw forces available, their readiness and the war scenarios, than from the models themselves. One recent article, perhaps the most optimistic assessment of all,[35] combines all of the critical assumptions needed for an optimistic assessment of the balance. These include slow reinforcement rates for the Warsaw Pact Category II and III units, akin to the rates shown in curve 4 of Figure 3; arrival rates for US reinforcements, especially US Reserve and National Guard units, similar to those of the Warsaw Pact Category II and III units, even though these forces must move over long distances inside the United States and by sea; additional credit to NATO for its assumed superior C³I and logistic support structure; a war scenario that implies a simultaneous start to the preparations for NATO and the Warsaw Pact, and that stretches over as long as three months. Almost regardless of the model used to evaluate the outcome of conflict, such input assumptions would almost certainly lead to a favourable result for NATO.

These models have taken the analysis of the balance in important directions. It is virtually impossible to understand the military problem faced by the West without taking into account the frontier of West Germany, its terrain features, requirements to provide a defence over that frontier, the advantages that NATO would have in a prepared defence position, and so forth. Some analysts have usefully sought to account for the ability of the Warsaw Pact to concentrate its attacks along a few selected axes and to predict the rates of movement, in order to be able to understand the effect on territorial loss for NATO, and they have engaged the question of the rates of attrition on the two sides. Although the results have often been skewed by the input assumptions, all these issues ought to be accounted for in analyses of the central front battle.

Experience with combat simulations shows that there are at least three other factors that must be treated carefully in any model – theatre and operational strategy, the breakthrough phenomenon, and air power. Theatre and operational strategy guide the initial decisions of the two sides on the allocation of forces – the choice of main attack axes, of defensive postures, of the withholding of reserves, of the operational posture of all the forces – and on the conduct of operations thereafter. The Warsaw Pact theatre commander, in particular, seeks to exploit breakthroughs and conduct large-scale manoeuvres in NATO's rear. The NATO commander, by the same token, wants to avoid this, and deploys his forces both to deny such success and, potentially, to mount counter-blows. Such decision-making needs to be replicated in a model of conflict.[36] Breakthroughs are a principal feature of Warsaw Pact operational strategy. In modern warfare, breakthrough attacks are the tried-and-true way to defeat an opponent.[37] War has been characterized by a sequence of battles, at all levels of warfare. Attackers sometimes succeed and sometimes fail. Military leaders seek to reinforce successes to create opportunities for new ones, hoping that one success will increase chances for success in the next battle, leading to a cascade of successes and a complete collapse of the defence in one or more key sectors. This would permit breakthroughs, rapid advances into the defence's rear area, and envelopments of major defence forces. Many models fail to capture these phenomena. They often implicitly treat the war as a single continuous battle and model the movement of the front on the average.[38] But war is not an average phenomenon. The result of each battle is uncertain. If the model treats the battle across the front as an average phenomenon, there would be high attrition and slow movement, but perhaps no breakthroughs. However, these could occur when the conflict is examined in a series of battles, creating opportunities for rapid movement and reduced attrition. Detailed combat simulations are needed to account for such discontinuous phenomena.

The role of air power is difficult to model. The close air support mission is the easiest, since it can be treated essentially as flying artillery. But air plays more roles, even in ground attack. Added to the close air support mission is interdiction behind the front lines, against both lines of communications and military units moving forward on them. History suggests that interdiction can play a crucial role in the outcome of the battle, not only by destroying forces but also by disrupting the attacker's plans, slowing the rate of reinforcement, and requiring readjustments, including even the halting of offensives. But the amount of air power available for ground attack depends on the result of an air war. Recognizing NATO's superiority in air power, the Warsaw Pact will seek to destroy NATO's air forces at their bases and, if that is not possible, in the air. By the same reasoning, NATO air force commanders will seek to protect their bases, to destroy Pact air power at its home bases if possible (offensive counter-air) and, if not, in the air (defensive counter-air). Once this is accomplished, NATO air forces can devote the bulk of their multi-role aircraft (those with ground attack and air defence capabilities) to ground attack missions. Combat models need to account for this complex air battle and capture the effect of air forces on the ground battle.

The assessment that follows is based upon a series of analyses employing a simulation of a theatre-wide conflict along the central front. In brief, the model covers a series of military activities. Military units on both sides mobilize, conduct training activities and move forward to assigned offensive or defensive positions. Theatre commanders choose strategies for their respective offensive or defensive postures – major axes of attacks, various defence preparations, and so forth. Attacks occur; military units engage, advance or retreat; they disengage, collapse, are annihilated or withdraw to cover exposed flanks. An air war is conducted, and the contribution of air forces to the ground battle is calculated. The rules adjudicating the results of combat are varied, favouring the defence in some situations (e.g., high defence density) and the offence in others (e.g., unprepared defences). As the battle unfolds, reserves on both sides are committed to shore up major axes of attack or to continue to hold the line. Because the war is fought at a theatre level, movement is depicted as the forward movement of the front line in nine sectors, corresponding to NATO's eight corps sectors and the Jutland sector in the north.[39]

In addition to their more comprehensive coverage of important military factors, such simulations provide a finer-grained picture of the potential outcome of combat than do the simpler models outlined above. The outcome can be depicted in several ways relevant to traditional measures of military success – seizure (or defence) of territory and destruction of enemy forces. With respect to the first, the simulation depicts the outcome of the battle in terms of territory lost and held, not only on an aggregate level but also providing geographic detail – the location of forces, their occupation of key strategic points (rivers, bridges, cities and towns) and their rates of movement. The simulation tracks overall attrition as an aggregate of the attrition suffered by individual combat units; individual units must withdraw from the battle when they have suffered too much attrition to continue to fight as a cohesive unit. Although the simulation is quite detailed, it can never be detailed enough. War is just too complex to model precisely.

Simulations are often used to assess the value of adding a specific capability to the NATO force structure, rather than to predict the outcome of conflict *per se*. In such 'marginal utility' analysis, comparisons are made between alternative programmes to improve NATO's military situation – for example, the value of adding a new air-to-air missile to the NATO inventory compared with adding (at the same cost) aircraft equipped with older air-to-air missiles. Without a simulation, analysts would typically estimate the number of enemy aircraft lost in combat, or the relative rates of attrition on enemy and friendly aircraft. But a simulation that can depict the relative value of such air improvements in terms of the outcome of ground combat would be more valuable for this problem, because it would account for the fact that the additional aircraft (but not the additional missiles) could also be used in ground-attack missions.

Analysts are well aware of the sensitivity of the results of such analysis to assumptions, and therefore they conduct sensitivity analyses. So long as the simulation is easy to use, numerous sensitivity checks can be made. In the marginal utility analysis, of course, the important question is whether the assessed difference between the two programmes is materially affected by the sensitivities.

Sensitivities are even more important when simulations are used to predict the outcome of a potential conflict. Analysts at RAND have made a detailed study of the sensitivity of simulation outcomes to uncertainties in the input assumptions,[40] revealing that there are two broad areas of uncertainty in the potential outcome of a war. The first, and more important, surrounds the scenario assumptions discussed above – the national commitments, the readiness of forces, and the relative preparation times. In general, these input assumptions, not the technical details of the model, have the larger effect on the results. For example, for most simulations based on the readiness assumptions depicted by curve 1 in Figs 3 and 4, NATO would be badly defeated. But for those based on the assumptions illustrated by curve 4, NATO forces would hold. And this only varies the assumptions concerning the treatment of readiness; changes in assumptions about national participation or preparation time have similar large effects.

The second area of sensitivity surrounds the technical details of the simulation, especially the assumptions concerning the adjudication of combat. For example, a change in the assumptions concerning the intensity of conflict can produce variations in the outcome. In general, greater intensity will lead to more rapid and decisive Warsaw Pact victories, whereas lower intensity will favour NATO. Similar sensitivities surround such factors as the assumed rates of advance, the force densities required to hold the front (the force-to-space ratio), and the assumed effectiveness of helicopters and air-to-ground munitions. These uncertainties affect the scale of a probable NATO defeat, but generally do not create a NATO victory. Only in scenarios where the Warsaw Pact fails to field the large or effective forces potentially available to it does NATO appear to have a substantial chance of holding most or all West German territory. The various technical uncertainties do not affect this basic point. Generally, NATO is successful in scenarios where East European forces fail to participate or perform very poorly. By the same token, NATO can hope for a successful forward defence when there is sufficient time available to deploy a large body of reinforcements from the United States, including those travelling by sea, and the Warsaw Pact does not deploy the strategic reserves of the high command.

A review of simulations in which NATO suffers varying degrees of defeat – ranging from the catastrophic to the less decisive, in which some West German territory is lost but NATO forces are not completely overrun – indicates that the most important factor in the balance is the relative availability of operational reserves on the two sides. Operational reserves obviously provide attrition fillers on both sides – forces to be put into combat when front-line forces have become exhausted. But Soviet operational strategy relies on operational reserves to nourish the main axes of attack, to build up large force ratios along those axes, to achieve breakthroughs and then exploit them. NATO's operational reserves need to be deployed in order to counteract this operational strategy.

In general, NATO forces suffer catastrophic defeats in the simulations when the NATO commander runs short of operational reserves and must begin to reduce the density of front-line defences. When a sufficiently strong defence can no longer be maintained along one of the Pact attack main axes, a breakthrough occurs. As that breakthrough is exploited, NATO forces must be withdrawn along a broad front, or are enveloped. The earlier that breakthroughs occur, the more rapid (and more decisive) the defeat. In simulations where the NATO commander is able to retain some operational reserve throughout the conflict without thinning his forward defences, his forces may be pushed back but are not seriously penetrated. When the NATO commander has a high level of operational reserves, NATO forces could hold a defensive line well forward for a considerable length of time.[41]

The dominant issue in the balance of forces in Central Europe is therefore the availability of forces for operational reserves on the two sides. This view of the balance is depicted in Figure 5 on p. 93,[42] which indicates the total number of DE available to the two sides over the course of a 30-day conflict in the 10/5 scenario. These forces stand roughly in a ratio of 2:1. Figure 5 also indicates the minimum level of forces needed to cover the front in a defensive posture. Estimation of such a minimum requires a detailed analysis of the terrain all along the front, since some terrain can be lightly defended (due to hills, lack of roads, etc.). Such terrain analysis leads to rules of thumb for the average minimum defensive forces needed to cover a front.

Figure 5: Simple view of the balance

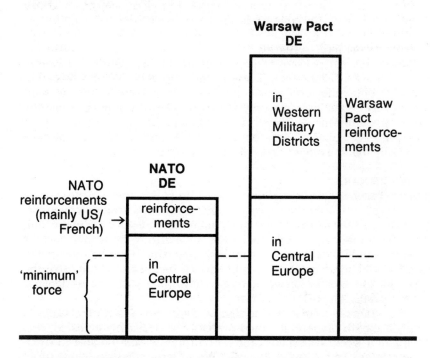

Contemporary estimates are normally around 25–30 km per division. These figures have grown since World War II, when the norm was around 10 km, as the range and firepower of weapons has increased.[43] The minimum force level shown in Figure 5 is based upon 30 km per division across a 650 km front.[44] Obviously the need to defend a longer front, as would be necessary to defend the Austrian frontier, would lead to a larger minimum force requirement. (The minimum force required to hold the front is, of course, not completely independent of the size of the opposing force. However, because the attacker has the initiative and can choose the time, place and size of his attacks, the defenders' minimum forces are more dependent upon the length of the frontage and the nature of its terrain than on the size of the opposing force.)

The ratio of forces in excess of the minimum available to defend the front is the most important single numerical factor in the balance of forces in Central Europe, not the overall force ratio. Those excess forces contribute to the imbalance in operational reserves, which is necessary for Warsaw Pact operational strategy to be successful. For the scenario indicated in Figure 5, this imbalance is roughly 4:1. The operational consequence of this imbalance is that the Warsaw Pact is able to create large local force advantages which are unpredictable by NATO in terms of both their location and their time of occurrence. These local superiorities can lead to breakthroughs, deep penetrations and, potentially, the collapse of the entire NATO defensive line.

Summing up: force scenarios
These points can perhaps best be understood by examining four potential scenarios for conflict. These do not represent actual simulation results, but rather are an attempt to summarize the lessons learned from various analyses in a structured way. The critical point is that the input assumptions – especially those connected to the scenario, not the model of combat – are the most important factors in balance assessments. It is these that define the ratio of excess forces.

A 5/1 SCENARIO
In a 5/1 scenario, Warsaw Pact forces attempt to achieve surprise. Five days probably provides adequate time to mount a major assault with forces in Eastern Europe, although many East European forces would not be completely ready. Follow-on forces from the western Soviet Union would barely have begun deploying, would not be fully ready, and would therefore not be immediately available to reinforce the assault. The attack plan would be a great gamble, with success depending crucially on NATO's reaction.

If NATO fails to react to the signs of an impending conflict and has only a day to prepare, it would probably be decisively defeated, perhaps in a week. Although some NATO forces would be able to reach their defensive positions along the West German border, they would not have time to prepare their positions. More important, many forces would not have time to reach their positions. Of course, US reinforcements, even air forces, would have no time to deploy to Europe, nor could France decide to commit its forces and send them forward.

Thus, Warsaw Pact forces would find huge gaps in the NATO defensive line and NATO defensive forces that were still in the process of getting organized. The result would probably be rapid, deep penetrations of the NATO defences and a quick decision.

This defeat might be averted by two more days of NATO preparation time. With this additional time, NATO forces would be in defensive positions, and large US Air Force reinforcements would have arrived, or would be close to arriving, at the opening of hostilities. A cohesive forward defensive line, even if not well dug-in, with strong air support, would have a good chance of holding off the initial assault. The Warsaw Pact would then be in deep trouble, because of the lack of immediate reinforcements from the Soviet Union. In fact, the risks of this scenario for the Pact cast doubts on its likelihood.

A 10/5 SCENARIO

In a 10/5 scenario, the Warsaw Pact would mount a major assault, again with the forces in Eastern Europe. But many of the follow-on forces from the Soviet Union would have already arrived, and others would be on the way, albeit at reduced readiness. The larger number of operational reserves at the outset would seem to make this a less risky scenario for the Warsaw Pact. For example, curve 3 in Figure 2 indicates that the Warsaw Pact would have about 42 DE, accounting for training readiness degradation – a force with 20 DE in excess of a minimum defensive level of 22 DE. During the following two weeks of conflict, around 20 DE would be added.

But the five days available to NATO in this scenario would also be important: the defensive line could be established cohesively and with a modest amount of preparation. US and French ground force reinforcements would be on the way, and US Air Force reinforcements would already be in place. NATO would have about 25 to 30 DE in place at the outset, with the number depending crucially on the speed of French commitment and movement and on that of US reinforcements. During the next two weeks, the level would rise into the mid-30s. The excess force ratio would be large at the outset, and, depending on attrition rates, NATO's small 'excess' could be whittled away faster than it could be replenished.

The Warsaw Pact would probably try to exploit the weakness of NORTHAG forces compared with CENTAG by creating major attack axes in the north while mounting pinning attacks against CENTAG forces. Although some US and French reinforcements would be able to reach the NORTHAG area as the conflict unfolded, their numbers might not be adequate over time, as Warsaw Pact operational strategy continued to wear down the defence in the north. To avoid serious breakthroughs, NATO forces must trade space for time, leading to a NATO withdrawal along a broad front and a substantial loss of NATO territory (e.g., 100–200 km) in that region over a few weeks.

Whether such territorial loss would be a decisive defeat is debatable. Warsaw Pact forces would not have achieved their military objectives, which would certainly include overrunning West German territory over the entire front and the destruction of the main body of NATO forces. In a military sense, this scenario does not depict the decisive military defeat. However, such a major loss of West German territory would be a political catastrophe for West Germany and NATO, and would not be conducive to a favourable post-war situation, to say the least. In political-military terms, such a territorial loss could easily be a decisive defeat of NATO, leading to its collapse.

A 10/5 SCENARIO (WITH PACT PRE-MOBILIZATION PREPARATIONS)
Perhaps as a consequence of a previous crisis, in this scenario the USSR would improve the training readiness of its forces in the western Soviet Union. Over a period of several months, soldiers would be called back into Category II and III divisions for individual and small-unit training and then be sent back home. The result would be a quantum improvement in the training readiness of those forces when mobilization occurred. Consequently, Warsaw Pact reinforcing forces would be far stronger after ten days of overt preparation than they would have been in the previous scenario. With reference to Figure 2 on p. 85, they would have moved from curve 3 to curve 1 – roughly 45 DE available at the outset, rising to 80 DE within the next week. This provides the Warsaw Pact with an overwhelming excess force advantage.

In this scenario, NATO either does not detect or fails to react to the Warsaw Pact 'pre-mobilization' training activities.[45] With five days to prepare, NATO forces would perform about as well against the initial Warsaw Pact assault as they did in the previous scenario during the first two weeks of the battle. However, when reinforcing forces from the Soviet Union began to enter the battle, they would be stronger than in the previous scenario and able to force more serious breakthroughs across the entire front, potentially leading to a complete collapse of NATO's defences.

A 20/25 SCENARIO
From the Warsaw Pact perspective, a 20/25 scenario is more conservative, since it allows the deployment of all reinforcements from the western Soviet Union before the outset of conflict, although some of those forces would still be at reduced readiness (see curve 3 in Figure 3 on p. 86).

But the time is more important to NATO. With three weeks of preparation, NATO forces on the front line would be well dug-in. All US POMCUS units would have arrived and deployed as operational reserves, as would all French units, if they had been committed to the Alliance. Simulations often indicate that, with the few more operational reserve divisions provided by POMCUS and careful preparation of the front, a grinding war of attrition is possible. This is by far the most favourable of the four scenarios from NATO's point of view. With a war of attrition and a slow-moving front, the Soviet Union would have to be concerned about defections among the East Europeans. But this could be changed, should the USSR decide to commit its strategic reserves to the battle.[46]

Conclusions
The imbalance of forces in central Europe favours the Warsaw Pact today. NATO would probably lose most war scenarios and be decisively defeated in many.

But the key word is 'probably'. As stated at the outset, the best that can be done is to predict the outcome, all other things being equal. They never are, of course. Despite analysts' efforts to include as many factors as they reasonably can – and modern conflict simulations treat a great many – they can never treat them all. Nevertheless, the essential fact of an imbalance of forces favouring the Warsaw Pact is inescapable.

But the analysis presented here indicates that 'fixing' the problem might not be too daunting a task. NATO's goal ought to be to reduce the feasibility, and therefore the likelihood, of the unfavourable scenarios. There is a broad range of potential measures,[47] but two categories stand out:

- Measures to provide a quick reaction to warning signals.
- Additional forces.

Reaction to warning signals is probably more important than the collection of them, because modern intelligence is likely to provide numerous indications of preparations for hostilities. The key is interpretation and political reaction. Ultimately, this is a question of political will, but some steps could be taken to improve NATO's ability to react, should crisis come – political involvement in exercises, improved communications and procedures, etc. Arms control might also play a role, by restricting important activities that must occur in war-preparation and thereby providing important indications of intent, should these restrictions be broken in a crisis. Whatever is ultimately done in this area cannot, however, really substitute for additional forces, because adequate reaction can never be assured.

Analysis[48] shows that force additions in the range of 5–15 DE would probably provide NATO with the capability to hold a Warsaw Pact attack in even the unfavourable third scenario discussed above. If the French commitment were assured, the range would be 5–10. It is possible that applications of advanced technology for interdiction, especially in the areas of intelligence, command/control and munitions, or improved forward defence preparations, such as rapidly created tank ditches and mines, would reduce these numbers further. Although the political obstacles to such force increases are high, these are *not* large numbers.

Because the numbers are not large, NATO has more leverage to improve its situation by its own unilateral actions than by arms control. The 'excess' Warsaw Pact forces are so large that they must be cut very deeply to have the same effect on the balance as the sort of additional NATO forces mentioned above: 20–30 Pact DE would need to be eliminated.[49] This suggests that arms control is probably not the best route to an improved conventional balance unless the USSR proves far more generous in future talks than it has been in the past.

In sum, the conventional balance is unfavourable to NATO. But large uncertainties cloud the assessment and make it difficult to be precise about the severity of the imbalance. Chief among these uncertainties are those associated with assumptions about the forces available to the two sides, the readiness of the forces, and the overall war scenario. Such input uncertainties are more important than the precise model of conflict, although this is also important. Modern combat simulations have underscored the importance of the breakthrough phenomenon and of the availability of operational reserves to the two sides. Indeed, the ratio of forces in 'excess' of those needed to provide a defensive cover of the front is a more valuable single index of the state of the balance than the traditional force ratio measure. The large number of these available to the Warsaw Pact, compared to NATO's relative paucity, is the chief source of NATO's conventional defence problem.

Notes

[1] The evolution and implementation of the forward defence strategy is discussed in Phillip A. Karber, 'In Defense of Forward Defense', *Armed Forces Journal International*, May 1984, pp. 27–50.
[2] CENTAG and NORTHAG are part of Allied Forces Central Europe (AFCENT). The Danish and German forces defending the approach to Jutland are part of Allied Forces Northern Europe (AFNORTH). The commanders of AFNORTH, AFCENT, and AFSOUTH report to the Supreme Allied Commander Europe (SACEUR). AFCENT's subordinate commands also include Allied Air Forces Central Europe (AAFCE), which provides air support to NORTHAG and CENTAG.
[3] Soviet operational strategy is detailed by John G. Hines and Phillip A. Peterson, *Soviet Strategy for Peace and War in Europe* (Los Angeles, CA: European-American Institute for Security Research, 1983).
[4] These figures are derived from *The Military Balance 1987–1988* (London: IISS, 1987). To reach the total number of divisions, a brigade or regiment is equated to one-third of a division. Naturally, these 'divisions' come in many sizes and shapes. French divisions, in particular, are far smaller than their American or German counterparts.
[5] The US Rapid Reinforcement Programme, which was part of the NATO Long-Term Defence Programme (LTDP). See Robert Komer, 'Is Conventional Defense of Europe Feasible?', *Naval War College Review*, September–October 1982, pp. 80–91.

[6] These second strategic echelon forces, plus the first strategic echelon, are considered to belong to the Soviet Union's Western Theatre of Military Operations (the acronym in Russian is TVD), *Soviet Military Power: An Assessment of the Threat 1988* (Washington DC: US Department of Defense, 1988), p. 14.
[7] Figures drawn from Michael Sadykiewicz, *Organizing for Coalition Warfare: The Role of East European Forces in Soviet Military Planning* (Santa Monica, CA: RAND Corporation, R-3559-RC, March 1988).
[8] 'NATO and the Warsaw Pact: Force Comparisons', NATO Information Service, 1984.
[9] Dale R. Herspring and Ivan Volgyes, 'The Political Reliability in the East European Warsaw Pact Armies', *Armed Forces and Society*, vol. 6, no. 2, Winter 1980.
[10] Zbigniew Brzezinski, 'White House Diary, 1980,' *Orbis*, vol. 32, no. 1, Winter 1988.
[11] Michael Sadykiewicz, *The Warsaw Pact Command Structure in Peace and War* (Santa Monica, CA: RAND Corporation, R-3558-RC, March 1988). Zbigniew Brzezinski, 'Peaceful Change in a Divided Europe', in Uwe Nerlich and James A. Thomson (eds), *Conventional Arms Control and the Security of Europe*, (Boulder, CO: Westview Press, 1988), pp. 15–27.
[12] The testimony of Col. Ryszard Kuklinski in the Polish-language journal *Kultura*, Paris, April 1987, pp. 3–57,

cited in both Sadykiewicz and Brzezinski (*op. cit.* in note 11). Kuklinski was a deputy head of the Operations Directorate of the Polish General Staff and chief of Strategic Defence Planning before November 1981.

[13] For example, on 12 December 1987 the French Prime Minister said that 'there cannot be a battle for Germany and a battle for France' and that, if West Germany were attacked, 'France's commitment would be immediate and unreserved' (*NATO Report*, 21 December 1987.)

[14] WEI/WUV stands for Weapons Effectiveness Indicator/Weighted Unit Value. The WEI score combines estimates of equipment firepower, mobility and survivability; these estimates are based upon a combination of physical data and military judgment. Judgments are also made about the relative importance of various categories of weapons, such as tanks or anti-tank weapons, in offensive and defensive operations. With these category weights, the scores are combined into the overall WUV score. William Mako provides the best description of this system: *US Ground Forces in the Defense of Central Europe* (Washington, DC: Brookings Institution, 1983). Unfortunately, as discussed by Barry R. Posen, Mako's data is based upon somewhat dated (1976) scores. ('Is NATO Decisively Outnumbered?', *International Security*, vol. 12, no. 4, Spring 1988, pp. 186–202; see footnote 12 in particular.) To account for the modernization of armouries, the WEI/WUV system has since been updated and the WEI/WUV used in the analysis in this Paper reflect contemporary scores.

The WEI/WUV system has been criticized over the years and does indeed have important failings. For example, it does not account for the effect of 'combined arms' – the value of an infantry unit does not depend solely on its weaponry, but also the quality of supporting armour, artillery and other forces. Despite admitted problems, however, there is currently no better system for accounting for the differences in quality among weapons.

[15] East European units are categorized by the same scheme but are at somewhat lower peacetime manning levels than Soviet units in the same category. See *The Military Balance 1983–1984* (London: IISS, 1983), p. 19.

[16] The US Department of Defense categorizes Soviet forces as ready, not ready (cadre), and not ready (mobilization). See *Soviet Military Power* (*op. cit.* in note 6), p. 89. According to David M. Shilling, the ready units correspond to Categories I and II and the cadre units to Category III ('Europe's conventional defence', *Survival*, vol. 30, no. 2, March/April 1988, pp. 126–7 and footnote 9).

[17] To give a rough estimate, assuming an average manning level of 40–50% and a total threat of 100–140 divisions, between 600,000 and 1,000,000 would be needed to flesh out the divisions alone, not to speak of the non-divisional support structure.

[18] According to *Soviet Military Power* (*op. cit.* in note 6, p. 89), the ready divisions (Category I and II) require only a 'brief' period of time; the cadre divisions, about a week, and the mobilization divisions, more.

[19] Posen (*op. cit.*, in note 14).

[20] *The Military Balance 1987–1988* (London: IISS, 1987), p. 228.

[21] Clearly the choice of the threshold is a matter of judgment, because a commander's judgment on whether to send less than fully ready troops to combat would depend on his needs. These will vary during the course of a conflict. For simplicity, I have chosen 70% for this analysis – a figure that splits the difference between the first and second approaches.

[22] Some aspects of support are replicated in the simulations discussed later in this Paper, specifically supplies and maintenance.

[23] Figures taken from Anthony H. Cordesman, 'Alliance Requirements and the Need for Conventional Defense Improvements', in Nerlich and Thomson (*op. cit.* in note 12).

[24] Steven Canby, *NATO Defense: What Can be Done*, 1986 (unpublished).

[25] Barry Posen (*op. cit.* in note 14) argues that NATO's larger support effort must have some value in combat. Accordingly, he increases the DE strength of NATO units by 50% in his

analysis. This is the equivalent of adding roughly 13 DE to NATO's existing force structure in Central Europe, with an equivalent percentage increase for reinforcing forces. It is no surprise, therefore, that Posen would find that the conventional balance is in equilibrium (if not in NATO's favour). Although he has raised an important point about the importance of the support structures, a more careful analysis needs to examine the alternative explanations mentioned in the text. Moreover, it would be preferable to treat the issues of the support structure directly in the analysis, rather than simply multiplying by a factor. Using simulations, to be discussed later, analysts currently seek to account for supplies and maintenance. Command, Control, Communications and Intelligence (C³I) are less well addressed.

[26] The actual time of travel would be much shorter. Assuming a conservative 40 km/hr for rail travel and an average trip of 1,500 km from the western USSR, rail travel time would be about two days. Combining this with other fairly conservative factors (a day each to load, transload and unload; a day to travel by road to the jumping-off position; and a day to organize for combat) leads to an estimate of a week. Harold Brown provided a two-week estimate, which presumably includes time to mobilize and allowance for rail and road capacity constraints (*Department of Defense Annual Report for Fiscal Year 1982*, p. 69).

[27] As with the Warsaw Pact times, the NATO figures can be derived from simple transportation planning figures. Forces in Central Europe must travel only a few hundred kilometres at most. Allowing a day each to load, move, unload and organize yields four days. The Rapid Reinforcement Program (POMCUS) is supposed to be implemented in ten days (see Komer, *op. cit.* in note 5), but this is based on such optimistic assumptions as the complete availability of divisions' equipment in POMCUS, clockwork operations by the European reserves supporting the effort, etc. More conservative assumptions would yield two to three weeks. Forces moving from the United States by sealift require additional time for mobilization and movement in the United States, as well as by sea, and they face rail, sealift, and port capacity constraints.

[28] These curves are based on the time estimates discussed above.

[29] Stephen Biddle shows that an attacker could gain a local superiority of 3:1 in one sector (out of a possible nine), with a force ratio as low as 1.25:1 (Stephen D. Biddle, 'The European Conventional Balance: A Reinterpretation of the Debate', *Survival*, vol. 30, no. 2, March/April 1988). The requirement for a 3:1 advantage for a successful attack also has murky origins in military history, but nevertheless seems widely accepted. A critique of this 'rule' can be found in Joshua M. Epstein, 'Dynamic Analysis and the Conventional Balance in Europe', *International Security*, vol. 12, no. 4, Spring 1988, pp. 154–65. See also Andrew Hamilton, 'Redressing the Conventional Balance', *International Security*, vol. 10, no. 1, Summer 1985, pp. 111–36, especially footnote 7.

[30] Hamilton (*op. cit.* in note 29, footnote 9), points out that support has been mustered for theatre-wide force ratio thresholds ranging from 1.2 to 2.0.

[31] Mako and Posen, (*opp. cit.* in note 14), and Posen, 'Measuring the European Conventional Balance: Coping with Complexity in Threat Assessment', *International Security*, vol. 9, no. 3, Winter 1985/1986, pp. 47–88. John Mearsheimer, 'Numbers, Strategy and the European Balance', *International Security*, vol. 12, no. 4, Spring 1988, pp. 174–85, and 'Why the Soviets Can't Win Quickly in Central Europe', *International Security*, vol. 7, no. 1, Summer 1982, pp. 3–39; Joshua M. Epstein (*op. cit.* in note 29); William W. Kaufmann, 'Nonnuclear Deterrence', in John D. Steinbrunner and Leon V. Sigal (eds), *Alliance Security and the No-First-Use Question* (Washington DC: Brookings Institution, 1983); Hamilton (*op. cit.* in note 29).

[32] The models of Posen ('Measuring the European Central Balance. . .', *op. cit.* in note 31) and Hamilton (*op. cit.* in note 29), for example, seek to account for force-to-space requirements, although in different ways and with different results.

[33] Kaufmann (*op. cit.* in note 31).

34 Epstein (*op. cit.* in note 29).
35 Posen (*op. cit.* in note 14).
36 Richard Kugler, 'Warsaw Pact Forces and the Conventional Military Balance in Central Europe', *Jerusalem Journal of International Relations*, vol. 8, no. 2–3, 1986.
37 *Ibid.*
38 Paul K. Davis, *The Role of Uncertainty in Assessing the NATO–Pact Central Region Balance* (Santa Monica, CA: RAND Corporation, P-7427, 1988).
39 Many of the conclusions presented here are based upon insights on analyses gained with using the RAND Strategy Assessment System (RSAS), in particular the part dealing with the central region. The RSAS is described briefly in Paul K. Davis, *Analytic War Gaming with the RAND Strategy Assessment System* (Santa Monica, CA: RAND Corporation, RB-7801, 1987). A fuller explanation of the theatre combat model is reported in Bruce W. Bennett, Carl M. Jones, Arthur M. Bullock and Paul K. Davis, 'Theater Warfare Modeling in the RAND Strategy Assessment System (3.0)', (Santa Monica, CA: RAND Corporation, N-2743-NA (forthcoming)).

In the model, units are tracked down to brigade (for NATO) or division (Warsaw Pact) levels. The strength of a unit depends on its DE score, which is adjusted to account for lack of training readiness, 'cohesion' and supplies. 'Cohesion' seeks to account for a unit's ability to conduct operations after suffering attrition; it can be improved by a period of recovery. Units are resupplied; damaged equipment is replaced from war reserve stocks or repaired.

The movement of units accounts for the time required to prepare for deployment from garrison or, for POMCUS units, to break equipment out of storage; for training to meet minimum standards of training readiness chosen by the analyst; and for movement along the rail or road network. Air interdiction can delay movement.

The analyst chooses the initial theatre and operational strategies for both sides. Thereafter, the simulation itself makes decisions about the allocation of reserves along major axes or to defence sectors according to a built-in set of rules. However, the analyst can intervene at any point.

A complex set of rules adjudicates the outcome of combat in any sector over periods (e.g., four hours) chosen by the analyst. The key factor is the ratio of strength of the units engaged in attack and defence in the sector. The total number of forces potentially in conflict is constrained by a 'shoulder-space' level chosen by the analyst. This force ratio is modified to account for terrain and other potential advantages to the defender. A set of equations calculates attrition to both sides in each of ten possible tactical situations. The equations are most favourable to the defence when it has had time to establish a prepared position, and most unfavourable to the defence during periods of breakthrough. The rate of movement of the front is similarly affected by the force ratio and the tactical situation; however, it is also greatly affected by the density of the defences. When the defence is strong, movement is slow; but when the defence slips below a density set by the analyst, the movement rate increases for a given force ratio and tactical situation. Again, during breakthroughs, movement rates are high. Air attacks also cause attrition and slow up movement. Finally, the simulation conducts air operations – offensive counter-air, defensive counter-air, and so forth – essentially to compute the number of ground attack sorties available to affect the outcome of the land battle.
40 The following discussion draws heavily on research conducted at RAND, especially by Paul Davis and Robert Howe. Also see Davis (*op. cit.* in note 38).
41 In many of the simulations that depict a defeat, the theatre-wide force ratio hovers around 2:1. Moreover, on a theatre-wide basis, attrition occurs at about a 2:1 ratio as well. This would seem to imply a stalemated outcome, because the two sides would fight to exhaustion in roughly the same amount of time. But in such situations this is usually not the result. The issues of defensive coverage of the terrain and the breakthrough phenomenon ultimately dominate. The attrition causes NATO to exhaust its operational reserves faster

than the Warsaw Pact; NATO's lines are thinned to compensate; Warsaw Pact attacks continue, and breakthroughs occur.

[42] James A. Thomson and Nanette C. Gantz, *Conventional Arms Control Revisited: Objectives in the New Phase*, (Santa Monica, CA: RAND Corporation, N-2697-AF, December 1987).

[43] For example, three US divisions and a cavalry group (roughly a brigade) were deployed in a defensive posture in the Ardennes in December 1944, covering a front of roughly 50 km from Mondshau to the Sûre River – roughly 15 km per division. These units were expected to hold their positions while the Allies mounted an offensive further to the north. They were, however, spread too thin and became the victims of the German offensive that broke through the American lines at the opening of the Battle of the Bulge. One division, seeking to hold 20 km, committed its reserves to hold the line but was penetrated across the breadth of the front. Its units were encircled locally and annihilated. (Author's analysis of information presented by Charles B. McDonald, *A Time for Trumpets: The Untold Story of the Battle of the Bulge* (New York: Bantam, 1984).)

[44] Some simulations, such as the CAMPAIGN model, in effect calculate such numbers by an examination of the terrain in each sector, which leads to a definition of the 'hold' density needed to maintain an effective defensive line, given the nature of the local defensive terrain. Such computations produce numbers close to the 30 km per division on the average.

[45] Failure to react is the more likely reason. Training preparations could easily be interpreted as innocuous. On the Western side, many would probably argue that the West need not take any important (or seemingly provocative) steps to react.

[46] As a general proposition, the more time available to NATO the better, so long as the USSR does not commit its strategic reserves. If the bulk of the US Army can get to Europe before the outbreak of hostilities, the Warsaw Pact would have a very difficult time. In such very long mobilization scenarios, there are grounds for agreeing with Joshua Epstein's statement that 'NATO has the material wherewithal to stalemate the Warsaw Pact' (*op. cit.* in note 29, p. 163). However, one must ask why the Warsaw Pact would attack under those scenario conditions when there are more favourable ones.

[47] See Davis (*op. cit.* in note 38).

[48] Thomson and Gantz (*op. cit.* in note 42).

[49] This difference in leverage can be illustrated arithmetically. If the key measure of the balance, the ratio of excess forces, stands at 60/15, then 5 additional DE added to the denominator have the same effect on the balance as 15 removed from the numerator. This is too simple but gives the general idea.

Arms Control: Problems of Success

PROFESSOR ADAM ROBERTS

Introduction
In the early 1980s, when some existing arms-control agreements were subjects of friction, when proposals for new accords were in trouble, and when the benefits of arms control were being questioned, many resisted the fashion and instead stuck obstinately to their arms-control guns. In particular, several writers (including some associated with the IISS) asserted that the factors which had led governments to take arms control seriously in the past were still very much in evidence, and that the approach to arms control which had emerged in Western Europe and the US around the time of the formation of this Institute would stage a come-back.[1] It has indeed done so, one might even say with a vengeance. Now, in the late 1980s, should a prudent analysis be that the pendulum will swing again, and that arms control will face serious difficulties in the next few years?

The central purpose of this Paper is to raise some awkward, but hardly new, questions about the value of arms control; and to suggest that formal arms-control negotiations and agreements may not be quite so appropriate a means of tackling the many urgent problems arising from arms competition in the contemporary world as today's conventional wisdom would have us believe. However, arms control has some significant achievements to its credit; some significant arms reductions are in train or under negotiation; and it is no part of this Paper's argument that arms control should be abandoned or even soft-pedalled.

Criticism of arms control, like arms control itself, has acquired some recognizable political overtones. It is associated, above all, with two distinct schools of thought, which can be crudely labelled Right and Left. Both have tended to see arms-control negotiations or agreements as being manipulated for the benefit of one government or another, rather than for a more general good. Both have expressed a preference for unilateralism – whether in arming (Right) or disarming (Left). Neither school of thought, at least in its politically influential form, has rejected all multilateral arms control, root and branch. To raise questions here about arms control is not necessarily to subscribe to either of these schools of thought; nor is it to suggest that arms control has reached a dead end, which it plainly has not; nor is it to assume that there is a single plainly superior alternative.

A number of lines of criticism of arms control deserve serious consideration at a time when the arms-control process is gathering pace. They include the argument that the burden of expectation being placed on arms-control talks is more than they can carry; that formal measures of arms control have too high a standing as the litmus test of the state of East–West relations; that some problems now being addressed in arms-control negotiations will not easily lend themselves to arms-control solutions; that the dynamic of arms-control negotiations, if not handled with extreme care, is such as to lead to a weakening of defence and deterrence; and that there has been a disproportionate academic and political emphasis on arms-control treaties, as distinct from some other approaches to the control and limitation of arms.

Arms control reborn
The revival of arms control in the late 1980s has been remarkable. The Stockholm accord of October 1986 and the Intermediate Nuclear Forces Treaty of December 1987 are the most concrete, but not the only, signs of this revival. There is also evidence of progress in several other East–West arms negotiations, whether on strategic arms reductions, conventional forces, or even chemical weapons.

Merely reaching agreements, or making progress in negotiations, does not in itself constitute success. What is impressive – so far – about both the Stockholm and the INF accords is the evidence of scrupulous observance on both sides. Moreover, the observation and inspection tasks outlined in these agreements have, up to now, been performed in an atmosphere verging sometimes on bonhomie. At long last the inspection hurdle has been decisively crossed – a simple fact which in itself opens up several important new avenues for arms control. The position is especially remarkable in the light of the Soviet Union's insistence over several decades that the one thing it could never contemplate accepting was inspection without disarmament: an exact description of what was agreed in Stockholm.

Furthermore, the Stockholm and INF accords mark a significant departure from previous accords in that they both involve Europe. In the past twenty-five years, European countries have generally been in favour of arms control – by others. Most have played a full part in such global arms-control regimes as the 1963 Partial Test Ban and the 1968 Non-Proliferation Treaty, and some European countries (including Finland and West Germany) have carried out those arms-control obligations imposed on them in the decade after the Second World War. However, by and large, Europe has presented an apparent paradox: an exceptionally stable continent, but one with little in the way of regional arms control.

On the part of the USSR, the rebirth of arms control has coincided with some significant departures from the language and practice of assertive unilateralism. The frequent appeals to interdependence, the talk of common security, and the acceptance that serious imbalances in forces need to be tackled, are all signs of a more multilateralist frame of mind – though the effect of this on the hardware and even software of the Warsaw Pact has yet to be made manifest. Perhaps the most concrete evidence so far of change in Soviet military policy is the beginning of the retreat from Afghanistan after almost nine years of involvement. One might even speculate that the USSR felt able to embark on this momentous course because it had begun, through the INF Treaty and other negotiations, to establish a steadier relationship with the US.

The US has also retreated from unilateralism, at least in its attitudes to regional conflicts and military projects. The Strategic Defense Initiative (SDI), initially presented as a unilateral protection from a threatening world (albeit one which might, implausibly, be shared with the USSR), has now become one more military project and claimant for a slice of the budget: the main focus of efforts to reduce nuclear dangers is again arms control, not particle beams and mirrors.

It is not just in the US and USSR that arms control in the late 1980s is doing reasonably well. Countries which in earlier periods were dismissive of arms control – China and France are the most striking examples – are now involved in negotiations at several levels. Even if they remain sceptical and cautious, they have acted in relation to some treaties, to which they are not parties, very much as if they were fully paid-up members: the Non-Proliferation Treaty is the obvious case in point. Moreover, the NPT, for all its known limitations, has attracted over 120 states parties, and has been observed better in its first twenty years than might have been predicted when it was concluded on 1 July 1968.

These developments are not all by any means new. Such phenomena as non-parties to an arms-control treaty observing its provisions, and unratified arms-control treaties being observed in practice, have been familiar parts of the scene for several years now – much to the despair, no doubt, of any pedants who would prefer a state's international legal obligations to be neat and unambiguous.

Although arms control should properly be seen as a permanent part of the practice of international relations, and not as a recent invention of liberals or socialists, there can be little doubt about the significance of changes in Soviet positions since 1985. If one had to identify one single factor out of the many which have contributed to the improved position of arms control in 1988, that factor would be Mikhail Gorbachev. His willingness to go beyond previous Soviet positions on the matter of inspection has revolutionized arms control in a very important way: certain types and degrees of disarmament – which Western states were not prepared to embark upon when satellite inspection, which suffers from certain well-known limitations, was the principal form of verification – have become at least conceivable. Moreover, to the extent that he has accepted the view of the Soviet

Union as a military giant and economic dwarf, Gorbachev has had a special incentive for putting emphasis on arms control.

It is true that many of Gorbachev's proposals (especially those in early 1986 for complete nuclear disarmament throughout the world by 31 December 1999) have not, apparently, been backed by any serious staff papers dealing with their more obvious difficulties. There has also been a lack of staff follow-up to some of his interesting statements about the need for new military doctrines, and about an enhanced role for the UN Security Council. His motives and methods are undoubtedly legitimate subjects for debate. Moreover, his most important moves in the arms-control field have had the character of finally coming round to long-held Western positions – whether on inspection, or on the zero option. All this said, the fact that Gorbachev has changed the arms-control landscape significantly can hardly be in doubt.

These developments are impressive as evidence of the obvious: that arms-control negotiations are likely to have a special importance in the next few years, and may well lead to significant new accords. In particular, there is clearly a prospect of a major US–Soviet reduction in strategic nuclear weapons; and even in the field of conventional arms in Europe there now appears to be more agreement in principle on how to proceed than there has been at any time since the MBFR talks started on 30 October 1973.

However, before such optimistic conclusions are accepted as the last word, it may be useful to remind ourselves of the problems which have long attended efforts in the arms-control field, and which are not likely to go away even in the improved atmosphere of 1988.

The problems of arms control: a historical perspective

Arms control, which can be found in one form or another in the history of most societies at most times, has had especially high international prominence throughout the twentieth century, both because of frightening developments in war-making capacities and because of the emergence of multilateral international conferences and agreements. The 1899 First Hague Peace Conference ushered in this new era of arms control and set a pattern which has endured: arms negotiations which often promise more than they deliver; Russia worried about the technological advantages of Western powers and anxious to be seen as a reformer of the international system; the US and the United Kingdom anxious not to jeopardize the fruits of their technical and industrial capacities. Some things do not change so very much in arms control.

A distillation of the problems and difficulties encountered in arms-control efforts throughout this century would include the following, which are germane to contemporary arms-control discussions.

– Arms control has in the past tended to go for the easy targets – especially for things which are easy to give up, or easy to verify, or both. So it has gone for nuclear tests rather than nuclear warheads –

except to the limited extent that the latter are covered by such existing agreements as the SALT II Treaty and the 1987 INF Treaty. Sometimes the easy targets are not the most important ones from the point of view of reducing international tension or preventing war. Thus the SALT I limits on the numbers of missiles, not accompanied by equivalent limits on multiple warheads, were a positive encouragement to develop such warheads. This was destabilizing, at least in the political sense that it was multiple warheads which gave some plausibility to the concern in the US in the late 1970s about a possible Soviet capacity to strike first at US nuclear forces. Qualitative developments and technological momentum present notoriously difficult targets for arms control.

- Arms control has focused attention on numbers to an excessive extent. If numbers had not become the currency for international negotiation it might matter less whether the US had 50% more, or fewer, nuclear weapons than the USSR. All numerical bargains require some assumptions to be made about the equivalence of the items which are being bargained away, but such assumptions are never easy even between two powers, and become much harder between more – whether at the level of warships, land forces, or even (at some point in the future) nuclear weapons.
- Arms-control agreements tend to get blamed for the underlying conditions which they in fact do little more than codify. Thus, in several countries (India being the most obvious), there is a tendency to attack the Non-Proliferation Treaty for establishing, hypocritically, a two-tier system of states. Likewise in the US the SALT treaties have been blamed (incorrectly in my view) for the fact that the Soviet Union has had some advantages in numbers or throw-weight in certain nuclear delivery systems.
- The ghost of general and complete disarmament, so firmly cast out by Hedley Bull and others over a quarter of a century ago, has come back to haunt arms control. It is all very well in theory to try to impose restraints, even reductions, on certain categories of weapon only, but it is extraordinarily difficult in practice. Military categories are not neat or self-contained: negotiations over one class of weapon, or one group of countries, always have knock-on effects on other weapons and other countries. Moreover, there is inevitably a political imperative for large and impressive schemes which offer the hope of freeing mankind from the shadow of war, as distinct from mere tinkerings and marginal reductions. Hence the absurdity that so many arms-control agreements, although products of a school of thought which self-consciously rejects general and complete disarmament, pay ritual obeisance to the latter in their preambles.
- Arms-control talks tend to be extremely arcane and slow. While it is easy to define the basic outlines of an agreement (whether it be a reduction of naval tonnage or of intercontinental missiles), working out the exact categories and conditions of a treaty on force levels is

fraught with difficulties. Negotiations are constantly at risk of getting overtaken by events, including changes in military technology and changes in the political environment. Thus, the preoccupations which led to a set of negotiations being embarked upon in the first place may have substantially changed by the time the negotiations are completed. The unratified SALT II Treaty was in part the victim of such a process.
- The long-standing question of the underlying purposes of arms control remains difficult. Such purposes as reducing the cost of mutual deterrence, reducing the danger of war breaking out at all, and reducing the destructiveness of war if it does break out, have frequently been advanced. They are valuable reminders that arms control is not a good in itself, but has to be judged in relation to some intellectually coherent criteria. However, it is notorious that these criteria may on occasion be mutually contradictory. Further, arms control often serves political purposes which are different from those advanced by theoreticians of the subject. It may be driven by a desire to reduce the danger of the peace movement, rather than of war; by a political requirement to stop a Mansfield resolution, rather than to actually reduce forces; by a wish to free a state's armed forces to deal with a third party; or by a political leader's need to be seen to be in charge and negotiating with major adversaries. Such purposes are perfectly understandable, even perhaps respectable, but they are necessary reminders that arms control may be the acceptable face of power politics, rather than a road to a better world.
- The records of government deliberations, if and when they are released, suggest that some arms-control and disarmament proposals need not be taken excessively seriously. Governments may be more dubious or divided about them than their public utterances at the time suggest. One illustration of this with an obvious contemporary resonance is the meeting between Churchill, accompanied by three other British ministers, and the Canadian cabinet in January 1952:

> When St Laurent asked whether the apparent concessions made by Russia about the banning of atomic weapons and the possibility of inspection indicated some desire to progress, Churchill replied with candour that it would be a difficult matter if the Russians accepted the west's conditions for control of atomic weapons, since the west was not strong enough to do without the protection of those weapons. Only the vast superiority of the US in atomic weaponry provided a decisive deterrent. However, it seemed doubtful whether Russia would allow a genuine and continuous inspection.[2]

- The compatibility between arms control on the one hand, and prevailing military doctrines on the other, is by no means easy to maintain, especially in a period which has been characterized, for better or for worse, by the dominance of deterrence based on offensive

nuclear forces. The weapons which cause the greatest public anxiety, or which are perceived as a threat by the adversary, are also in many cases the very weapons which are viewed by governments or strategic experts as the main foundation of international security. Thus arms control and strategy, supposedly compatible, find themselves in an uneasy relationship with each other – as the nervous post-INF Treaty utterances of strategic analysts on the subject of short-range nuclear forces show.
- Arms control is capable of dealing with problems which have at least some elements with a symmetrical character, such as the nuclear forces of the super-powers, but it is not necessarily so effective in tackling the great variety of problems which lack any such character. Thus, discussions on conventional forces in Europe have always run into difficulties not just because of the fundamental asymmetry between East and West in the matter of conventional force levels, not just because of such technical asymmetries as the difference in size and structure between a Soviet division and a NATO division, and not just because the possible missions of a Soviet division in Eastern Europe are internal as well as external: it is also because on each side of the East–West divide each government approaches the whole subject of conventional arms control with different interests, hopes and fears.
- Arms control, by its very nature, deals in a technical way with armaments, yet inevitably other political and foreign-policy issues impinge on negotiations. They often do so in a confused and messy way. The discussions in the 1970s about linkage between arms control, on the one hand, and Soviet internal policies as well as foreign involvements, on the other, were an example of such difficulties. These discussions, while reflecting a real problem, suffered from the defect that one super-power was hardly likely to allow itself to be coerced in major policy matters by another, nor indeed was the interest in arms control so asymmetrical that one side could hold out for major concessions on other issues, or the other side feel obliged to make those concessions.
- The observance of arms-control agreements frequently causes problems. This is not only because of deliberate and large-scale violations, which are a rarity. Legal measures of avoidance are a more serious problem. Pocket battleships in the 1930s, multiple warheads in the 1970s, and SS-20s in the 1980s, have all been perfectly legal means of ensuring that arms control affecting one category of weapon was compensated for by arms build-up in a very closely related category. Furthermore, some deployments and actions in the strategic sphere are by nature thoroughly ambiguous: witness the different Western interpretations of Soviet reasons for constructing, and plans for operating, the Krasnoyarsk radar. The prohibitions on the stockpiling and use of biological weapons have also been followed by a number of disputes about possible and actual violations:

however, the US accusation of deliberate use of 'Yellow Rain' in Indochina by North Vietnam or its allies appears to have been based on hasty political judgments and is now in the process of being quietly dropped.

Prospects for future agreements
What light, if any, does the preceding litany of difficulties of arms control shed on the prospects for future progress in this field?

Much of the contemporary diplomacy of arms control is being conducted on both sides by highly professional negotiators, to whom the difficulties recited here would present no surprises. There has been much evidence of awareness of the need to proceed cautiously. On the Western side at least, arms control is now the subject of somewhat less inflated rhetoric and exaggerated expectations than was the case, say, fifteen or twenty years ago.

The reasons for seeking arms control remain compelling: the Soviet Union needs to restructure its whole economy in a less heavily military direction, and although arms-control accords can only play a very modest part in this gargantuan task, if they help at all they are likely to be pursued. For its part, the US too is conscious of over-extension, and an improved relationship with the USSR may help to lower the costs of commitments, not just in Europe, but also in relation to some of the regional conflicts around the world. In Europe, there is a very strong interest in tackling various aspects of the conventional arms confrontation – even if there are different views as to which aspect should have priority. This conjunction of solid interests in favour of arms control is remarkable.

One further factor might, but only might, powerfully assist the cause of arms control. If the Soviet Union were seen to be moving away from the crusading spirit, if it were clear that it is judging the value of foreign involvements by sensible economic yardsticks, and if it took significant steps towards the acceptance of pluralism both at home and abroad, then some of the ideological fervour which has sustained confrontation and inhibited arms control could abate. There is a great deal of evidence that the Soviet Union is moving in these directions. However, a note of caution is needed here. Scepticism about the likely destination of the Soviet reforms is still justified.

One version of scepticism has been put in paradigmatic form by Caspar Weinberger. He has expressed the view, also advanced at times by Henry Kissinger, that the USSR may be reforming economically in order all the better to weaken the West. He has associated *perestroika* almost entirely with economic, as distinct from political, reform; he has referred to 'the fundamental and unchanging nature of the Soviet system'; and he has said that 'no General Secretary will be allowed to alter in any fundamental way the never-changing goal of world domination, or the nature of the Soviet regime'.[3] There is an element of dogmatism in such a view, and a failure to explain why the USSR should, perhaps uniquely, be incapable of abandoning a presumed goal which is as unattainable as it is undesirable.

Another form of scepticism, much more persuasive, is almost the opposite. In this version, the economic reforms are not likely to have any dramatic success, so – even if there was an idea of eventually burying the West – it is incapable of realization. On the other hand, the decline of the Communist faith, especially in its Messianic aspects, is likely to continue; and some of the many political and foreign-policy changes initiated by Gorbachev may well endure. All this is not necessarily a cause for celebration: these changes could lead to serious instabilities within the USSR and Eastern Europe; and in any case it is unwise to assume that relations between great powers are by nature good, and have only been difficult between the US and USSR because of the ideological factor.

Looking at the individual sets of arms-control negotiations currently taking place or planned, one is bound to be struck by the difficulty of some of the issues which have to be faced.

The START talks are the most likely candidate for producing an early agreement, and a 50% reduction in the huge intercontinental nuclear arsenals of the two sides hardly seems dangerous or revolutionary. Yet, although the shape of an agreement is clear, to move from an outline to a definite treaty is a huge step. There is evidence of hesitation on both sides about taking it quickly. Related issues – whether anti-ballistic missile systems or sea-launched cruise missiles – are rearing their ugly heads. If nuclear forces are to be reduced, there may be a need for constraints on the technologies which could, at some future date, threaten the utility of such forces.[4] The conclusion and implementation of a START accord is not going to be easy: it lacks the comparative simplicity of the INF Treaty.

Further constraints on nuclear testing are clearly a possibility. They would not have any very dramatic effect in curbing East–West arms competition, but they would be useful as an outward and visible sign that the super-powers are serious about arms control and willing, however belatedly, to do something to keep their part of the Non-Proliferation Treaty bargain.

The negotiations towards a chemical weapons disarmament agreement have made remarkable progress, but the subject remains very difficult. Verification, always problematical in this area, might have to be so intrusive that it opens up possibilities of industrial espionage. It is no accident that chemical weaponry has traditionally been tackled indirectly: by the 1925 Geneva Protocol's prohibition on use, rather than by a more typically arms-control approach of addressing the legality, or levels, of possession. The prohibition on use is certainly fragile, as the events of the Iran–Iraq War have shown. But it may have to remain the principal formal barrier to chemical warfare.

The planned Conventional Stability Talks (CST) in Europe present the most intellectually challenging opening for arms control. Nothing in the past record of negotiations about conventional disarmament – whether in the 1930s, or in the MBFR talks – could encourage optimism. There is even a risk that for the Soviet Union these talks could serve the function which the MBFR talks served for the United States – that of putting off the evil day when unilateral force reductions are undertaken. On the Western side, there has been an impressive degree of official preparation for these talks, but it remains far from obvious what items might be sacrificed in order to get Soviet reductions, and the talks will raise touchy questions about what kind of European military order is really wanted by the Western powers. Yet there is bound to be a wide measure of agreement on the reduction of capacities for surprise attack by land forces.[5] Moreover, the extent to which the Soviet side has adopted a flexible posture in relation to these proposed talks is remarkable: it is evidently prepared to exchange data, to verify it, and – most important, if it can be done – at least to consider removing asymmetries.

In the eyes of some, the real Soviet objective in conventional arms talks is the establishment of a political and diplomatic framework for a wide-ranging debate on European security.[6] If this is so, it is an interesting question whether such a debate should be welcomed or not. There is a long history of Soviet proposals for a European security system, going back to at least the early 1950s: their hidden agenda may have included the departure of the Americans and the denuclearization of Europe. Yet it is not clear that this has been the only view in the Soviet Union, then or now: there is also some evidence to support the contentions that some Soviet leaders have seen certain advantages in the system of alliances built up in Europe over the past forty years, and that they have reasonable suggestions to make about the future of that system. The common characteristic of Soviet proposals in this area, not overcome today, has been vagueness. Yet, precisely because of this defect, Western powers have been able to take up the idea of European security and inject into it their own clear conceptions of the prerequisites of stable relations – a task which they accomplished fairly effectively in the 1975 Helsinki Final Act, and which they might well attempt to repeat in any future negotiations about security matters.

Conclusion: the need for complementary approaches
There are indeed prospects for further arms-control accords in the near future, both in the nuclear and conventional fields, but they are for accords which raise difficult problems. It is not just that their terms are complex, nor that they tie in to already touchy debates within the Western Alliance about such matters as burden-sharing. It is also that arms control seems sometimes to lurch from one subject to another, with too little time to reflect on the kind of criteria which should guide it, or the kind of security system which should emerge at the end of the process.

Whether we are really moving from a world of arms control to one of arms reduction on a large scale may be doubted. Of course, the classical concept of arms control has always encompassed the idea of reductions, but until the INF Treaty (and possibly START) there was not much progress on that front. Actual reductions are probably easier in respect of nuclear weapons (not least because of the gross oversupply at present) than in respect of other weapons. Even in this area, the prospect of serious and lasting reductions is far from certain: the fissile material from dismantled weapons, returned to central casting, may yet reappear in new roles. Moreover, even in many areas involving nuclear weapons, including sea- and air-launched cruise missiles, arms control may not involve actual reductions but rather limitations on future growth and deployment.

The present revival of arms-control discussions may have an inherent value, irrespective of whether any new arms-control treaties are concluded. The fact of holding arms-control talks at all can itself constitute welcome recognition that security is a problem which, to an extent at least, needs to be addressed in a multilateral framework. Moreover, arms-control talks can be a useful vehicle for enabling each side to understand the other's security concerns and rationales. Finally, they can lead to valuable confidence-building measures, even if they do not lead to any formal restrictions on the manufacture, possession and deployment of arms.

Impressive as the recent revival of arms-control dialogue is, multilateral measures of arms control should not have a complete monopoly of attention. Like all approaches to security problems, arms control suffers from certain defects. To concentrate excessively on formal East–West arms-control measures may be to face important contemporary problems unprepared. A few may be mentioned:

- In the forthcoming Conventional Stability Talks, the question of cutting those types of forces with invasion potential will certainly be raised, but NATO has never itself systematically addressed the question of shaping conventional forces so that they convey a manifestly defensive message. This is a question which should be addressed first and foremost as a defence matter, and only later as an arms-control one. It is a very difficult question for NATO, with its reliance on a nuclear retaliatory capacity and mobile armed forces, yet elements of this approach to defence problems have a respectable lineage and a strong political appeal. It is hard to imagine NATO's strike aircraft can be kept out of serious negotiations for long.
- Despite the known weaknesses of unilateralist positions, it remains the case that not all arms issues are best tackled in bilateral or multilateral negotiations. There remains scope for states to make changes in their arms policies on a more or less unilateral or intra-alliance basis. A commonly cited example is the possible withdrawal of Soviet troops from some Eastern European countries. It may make

sense for the Soviet Union to pull troops out unilaterally – or by agreement with the governments of the countries concerned. It is an interesting question how NATO would respond to a large-scale and permanent withdrawal along these lines.
– During the Iran–Iraq War, the prohibition of use of chemical weapons has been violated on a large scale by Iraq. This action, undermining the important restraint on the use of such weapons in the 1925 Geneva Protocol, met only limited opposition from the major powers. The implications for other arms-control and laws-of-war regimes may be serious. The matter deserves at least as much academic and official attention as do some of the more fashionable topics of arms-control discussions. Maintaining old agreements and prohibitions may be as important as embarking on new measures of arms control.
– As the East–West conflict has declined in intensity, conflicts involving third-world countries have shown few signs of alleviation. If arms-control regimes are effectively to involve such countries, it will have to be on the basis of recognizing that the problems they face are quite different in character from those of the central East–West balance. Any arms-control regime which gives the appearance of being forced on third-world countries by the major powers is likely to prove fragile. Limitations on such issues as the supply of ballistic missiles to third-world countries may be necessary, but they are not a substitute for regional and bilateral agreements, or indeed for global agreements in which third-world countries feel they have a stake.
– For better or for worse, those whose main job it is to pare national budgets down are likely to remain, as they have always been, the most important arms controllers. It may well be that such ambitious schemes as the Strategic Defense Initiative will be more susceptible to this kind of control than to any new formal international agreement on top of the already-existing limits imposed by the 1972 ABM Treaty.
– On some matters, not limited to chemical weapons, restrictions on use may be as important as the more typical arms-control approach of restrictions on manufacture, testing and deployment. NATO, obsessed by the major issue of nuclear deterrence, has been woefully disorganized in its consideration of such matters – witness the fact that only six member states have become parties to the 1977 Geneva Protocol I on international armed conflicts, while the remainder have not – at least not yet.[7]
– The preoccupation with formal measures of arms control may also have deflected attention from the vital matters of rules of engagement, national legal frameworks for the use and control of armaments, and the choice of weapons systems which are stable in crises and discriminate in use. These matters have all been raised sharply by the 1983 Korean and 1988 Iranair airliner disasters.

The approaches hinted at here cannot be a complete substitute for arms control of more familiar kinds, if only because there are always some arms issues that can only be dealt with by formal peacetime restrictions on a multilateral basis. However, at a time when it is again at the centre of the stage, when it is one focus of a much larger shift in relations between the USSR and the West, and when it is cast in its old role of a litmus test of the state of East–West relations, it may be well to recall the limits of arms control as well as its strengths.

Notes

[1] Among them, Lawrence Freedman, 'Arms Control: On the Possibilities for a Second Coming', paper presented at the Millenium Conference, London School of Economics, April 1980; and Hedley Bull, 'The Classical Approach to Arms Control Twenty-three Years After', first published in Uwe Nerlich (ed.), *Soviet Power and Western Negotiating Policies*, vol. 2, (Cambridge, MA: Ballinger, 1983). A contrary view, that 'arms control negotiations are likely to be of little utility in the coming decade', was expressed by Richard Burt, 'International Security and the Relevance of Arms Control', paper for the 1980 Millenium Conference, p. 6.
[2] David Dilks, '"The Great Dominion": Churchill's Farewell Visits to Canada, 1952 and 1954', *Canadian Journal of History*, vol. XXIII, April 1988, p. 55.
[3] Caspar W. Weinberger, 'Arms Reductions and Deterrence', *Foreign Affairs*, Spring 1988.
[4] A point made by Ian Bellany in 'START and Stability', *The Council for Arms Control Bulletin*, no. 38, London, June 1988.
[5] On the question of developing force structures with less by way of invasion capability, the European neutral and non-aligned states have a contribution to make. Some of their representatives have expressed understandable concern that the structure of the conventional talks might prevent them from making it. See Carl Lidgaard, chief Swedish representative at the CSCE follow-up meeting in Vienna, 'Disarmament: Give These Countries a Hearing', *International Herald Tribune*, Paris, 22 April 1988.
[6] This view of Soviet objectives was advanced by Benoit d'Aboville, Deputy Political Director, Ministry of Foreign Affairs, Paris, in 'The Atlantic Alliance and the Problems of Disarmament', *NATO Review*, Brussels, vol. 36, no. 2, April 1988, p. 21. His critical view of the conventional force negotiations is partly based on a rejection of any idea of conventional deterrence (p. 19).
[7] As at 1 July 1988, the six NATO member states which have ratified the 1977 Geneva Protocol I are Belgium, Denmark, Iceland, Italy, the Netherlands and Norway. All have entered reservations, in some cases relating to nuclear deterrence. Details in A. Roberts and R. Guelff, *Documents on the Laws of War*, 2nd edn., revised (Oxford: Oxford UP, forthcoming, 1989).

From Arms Control to Arms Reductions: Achievements and Perspectives

AMBASSADOR GERARD C. SMITH

Introduction
This Paper focuses on the issues of controlling strategic and intermediate-range nuclear forces. It first briefly reviews the arms-control record, then discusses the INF Treaty and the prospects for START. The Paper concludes with a few thoughts that may be helpful in guiding future efforts.

The arms-control record
The record of arms-control successes is more extensive than generally realized. Since 1959, when the Antarctic Treaty – the first US–Soviet arms-control treaty – was signed, the super-powers have been parties to no fewer than 18 arms-control agreements. Five have limited the spread of nuclear weapons to other countries and banned them from particular environments, such as outer space and the ocean floor; six have focused on measures such as the Hotline to reduce the risk of nuclear war; three have limited nuclear testing; three have constrained strategic offensive and defensive arsenals; and the most recent accord will eliminate ground-based intermediate-range missiles. Of these agreements, almost all are of indefinite duration and remain in full legal effect.

Taken together, these agreements comprise an arms-control regime robust enough to have weathered the shifting political winds of three decades. This regime has done much to introduce predictability into the US–Soviet nuclear competition, adding a measure of stability to the strategic balance that would have been absent had the arms race proceeded unfettered. It has also institutionalized procedures to improve US–Soviet communication and the transparency of their military activities in an effort to lessen the risk of nuclear war. Finally, this regime has laid the groundwork for substantial weapons reductions and has helped foster what has become a fairly widespread belief: that regulating the strategic arms competition is essential to the emergence of any lasting US–Soviet co-operative security regime.

Over the years, however, the commitment of the parties to these agreements has waxed and waned, making the overall record of arms control somewhat spotty. On three occasions the United States failed to ratify treaties it signed. As a result, the 1979 SALT II Treaty, the

1974 Threshold Test Ban Treaty, and the 1976 Peaceful Nuclear Explosions Treaty never entered into force, although their provisions (up until recently in the case of SALT II) have generally been observed. In the last eight years, the erosion and abandonment of existing agreements has weakened a treaty regime painstakingly constructed by six US Presidents. The Reagan Administration's decision no longer to be bound by the terms of SALT II scuttled the only negotiated constraints on US and Soviet strategic nuclear forces. And the 1972 ABM Treaty, whose premise remains a *sine qua non* for substantial reductions in the offensive forces of the two sides, has been threatened by this Administration's second thoughts about the destabilizing nature of strategic defences. Two developments in particular – the pursuit of a crash programme (SDI) to develop and deploy nationwide defences as soon as possible, and the cavalier claim that the ABM Treaty has a much broader interpretation than that which the Senate was advised during the ratification process – have cast doubt on the US commitment to arms control in general. The stability of treaties is an essential element both in the stability of the strategic balance and in the future of arms control. To denigrate or breach existing bargains is certainly a poor way of laying the ground for new ones.

The super-powers' commitment to arms control has also been shaken by repeated rumblings over treaty compliance. In the Reagan years, the United States has ceased to deal constructively with legitimate compliance concerns. The once-productive Standing Consultative Commission has been supplanted by a public-relations campaign designed to advertise, rather than resolve, alleged violations. Although the Soviet compliance record has been less than perfect – especially in the construction of the large Krasnoyarsk radar situated in a manner prohibited by the ABM Treaty – the US government's handling of this and other compliance issues suggests that it may have been more interested in questioning the arms-control structure than in bringing the Soviet Union into line with its treaty commitments. The United States has also trumped up violations charges that are at best militarily insignificant and at worst totally groundless. Not surprisingly, the USSR has retaliated with similar charges of American violations. The crossfire has hardly improved the climate for negotiations.

Furthermore, in the past several years arms control seems to have strayed from its original path, neither informed by an overriding logic nor suggestive of a clear American concept of where the process should lead. As an example, after American insistence that nationwide ABM systems would be destabilizing, the Soviet Union accepted the strict limitations of the ABM Treaty; but now the US is pressing to decontrol defensive systems, even at the risk of losing a Soviet commitment to reduce sharply its retaliatory forces. Somehow the illogic of trying to control offensive weapons while planning to build a nationwide defensive system has escaped US leaders.

Recently, the United States has put targets of opportunity before clarity of purpose. How did it happen that a treaty controlling the middle section of the nuclear weapons spectrum, the INF weapons, was the first to be completed? Logically, one would have thought that the first priority would be to reduce strategic systems, and only then intermediate systems, and finally tactical forces. Perhaps the INF Treaty was just a case of taking what we could get at a time when US insistence on building nationwide strategic defences was blocking movement toward the control of strategic offences.

The INF Treaty
As the most notable US–Soviet arms-control achievement in the last eight years, the INF Treaty deserves comment. Most observers would undoubtedly agree that the Treaty is more important politically than militarily. It gives a positive thrust to arms control in general, placing a US Administration with a conservative ideology in the position of enthusiastically endorsing a process which so many of its members appeared for so long to suspect. The Treaty and its ratification have done much to reinvigorate bipartisan support for arms control as a key component of national security policy. In the longer term, it may also prove to be an important step in improving political relations between the super-powers. The INF Treaty also marks a transition from arms limitation to arms elimination, as well as a new Soviet acceptance of asymmetrical reductions down to equal levels. In this regard it is bound to set a good precedent for future negotiations, especially for conventional force reductions.

The Treaty's military significance is more limited. It requires only a minimal reduction of the sides' overall nuclear weapons arsenals – about 4% – and it leaves unbanned large numbers of weapons which can hit the very same targets at which the INF systems were aimed. With strategic forces unconstrained, and modernization planned for our theatre nuclear forces, the Treaty's military impact may well diminish over time. For some time the US has been seeking to lessen reliance on strategic systems to deter Soviet aggression against Western Europe. But it seems that in agreeing to destroy our INF forces we may have increased our reliance on strategic forces for that purpose. Whether or not this proves to be the case depends on what NATO does to improve the balance of conventional forces in Western Europe, either unilaterally or by agreement with the Warsaw Pact.

Nevertheless, the elimination of ground-based INF missiles should improve crisis stability in Europe. For nearly ten years the United States and its Western allies have focused attention on Soviet INF systems – especially the SS-20 – as a primary threat to Europe. And the Soviet Union has thought (with some justification) that the short flight time of the *Pershing II* posed a prime threat to Soviet authorities, giving them little or no warning of attack. The elimination of these systems will not be without strategic and psychological impact.

The INF Treaty's comprehensive and highly intrusive verification provisions are especially noteworthy and constitute a genuine breakthrough. A more concrete example of *glasnost* would be hard to find. For decades the Soviet Union resisted this degree of on-site inspection. But, in the wake of the recent spate of cheating charges, some amount of on-site inspection was certainly a political requirement. Soviet acceptance of such an intrusive human presence inside Soviet facilities marks a major turning point in arms control. We are presented with a powerful new tool for monitoring future agreements, one which will shape our choices about what to limit and how. (Perhaps if we had had on-site inspection in 1970 the disastrous deployment of MIRV would have been avoided, and strategic stability would now be very much better.)

But on-site inspection should not be viewed as a panacea for verification problems and compliance concerns. The burden of gathering essential information will continue to rest on national technical means – photo-reconnaissance satellites and the like. In fact, I doubt whether the full array of inspection measures that make the INF Treaty such difficult reading are really necessary, or will assure the United States that the Soviet Union is in full accordance with the Treaty's constraints. I also suspect that, after an early period of enthusiasm for this novel form of Soviet-American military co-operation, we may become a little less starry-eyed about the endeavour. Either we will be looking for ways to cut the costs and inconvenience of constantly checking each other's facilities, or we will be harassing each other about alleged failures to comply with every detail of an extremely complex inspection protocol. Even if the substantive bans on INF systems are honoured, squabbles over the minutiae of the inspection regime may end up replacing the cheating charges of an earlier era. Over time, we will also be required to assess the psychological effects of the pervasive presence of Soviet inspection officials in the United States.

Prospects for START
It now seems clear that a new President will be in the Oval Office before a START treaty is completed in Geneva. Some have speculated that the Soviet Union would like to have had Ronald Reagan, a President with impeccable conservative credentials and the first in 16 years to have an arms-control treaty ratified by the US Senate, sign the agreement. But, as the American election nears, the chances of getting a START treaty in 1988 dwindle. At the time of writing (Autumn 1988), they are virtually zero. It is, however, probably safe to predict that a START treaty will be signed by the next President, be he Bush or Dukakis.

Unlike the INF Treaty, a START agreement would reduce Soviet forces that directly threaten the US deterrent – particularly systems, like ballistic missiles, which are capable of carrying out a surprise attack. Although overall reductions will be of the order of 30% (rather than the 50% advertised), the Soviet Union has agreed to halve its aggregate throw-weight and its numbers of heavy land-based missiles. The START counting rules will also provide the USSR with incentives to increase its reliance on relatively slow-flying bombers and cruise missiles, which are less threatening.

The most essential condition for the success of START is the maintenance of the ABM Treaty, as traditionally interpreted, as the foundation on which to build. The United States and the Soviet Union must come to some understanding about strategic defences – an understanding which will sustain and, I hope, strengthen the ABM limitations already in place. In pursuing strategic defence research and development, both sides should be vigilant in guarding against two types of activities: outright violations of the ABM Treaty, and activities that stretch the meaning of the Treaty's terms to breaking point. If we fail to preserve the ABM Treaty, it is probable that START reductions will not be implemented, even if a treaty is signed.

It is now being said that the Soviet perception of SDI as a threat has lessened, as the programme's technical promise wanes and as the US Congress tightens its purse-strings to keep the Administration from implementing a looser interpretation of the ABM Treaty. But in the long run I doubt whether the USSR will rely on Congressional action to contain American strategic defences. As I see it, the Soviet Union will either continue to condition its agreement to deep cuts on some US commitment not to test and deploy nationwide defences, or it may make a commitment to reduce its retaliatory forces, but slow up or avoid its implementation until the fate of SDI becomes clear. Whether SDI will ultimately be a bargaining chip in negotiations, an insurance policy against the risk of Soviet break-out from the ABM Treaty, or something more sinister, its continuation in its present form is fundamentally incompatible with the aim of sharp offensive reductions.

If and when a START treaty is signed, it will have a profound impact on decisions about the structure of US strategic offensive forces. Although many details of the treaty have yet to be pinned down, the basic provisions to which both sides have already agreed suggest that Pentagon planners will have to operate under very different constraints in a START environment. For the first time, they will have to work with a finite budget of strategic warheads. Modernization, to the extent that it occurs, will be synonymous with replacement, rather than expansion. This fact alone will render a START treaty truly historic, whatever its other attributes.

Limiting the strategic offensive arsenal in this manner will induce hard, but ultimately healthy, trade-offs between and within the various legs of the triad. START will also change some of the force planning incentives and disincentives established by SALT I and II. By primarily constraining launchers, SALT did not discourage putting the largest number of warheads permitted into a limited number of delivery vehicles. But by primarily constraining warheads, START encourages each side to put its strategic eggs in a greater number of baskets, within the 1,600 launcher limit, in order to enhance the survivability of a smaller triad. Under START, missiles with one or just a few warheads make the most strategic sense.

START is unlikely to result in any significant redistribution of warheads between the various legs of the triad, in unanticipated or unwanted retirements on any large scale, or in force-structure decisions that did not already need to be taken. Nevertheless, the conclusion of a START treaty can be expected to bring the most difficult and contentious issues surrounding each leg of the triad into sharper focus. Although the treaty is unlikely to raise fundamentally new questions, it may force the resolution of long-standing dilemmas.

For the land-based leg of the triad, START will intensify the debate about ICBM vulnerability, encourage a reassessment of heavy MIRVing, and force a decision (if one has not already been taken) on a mobile ICBM. For the sea-based leg, START will mean a re-examination of US submarine survivability in the context of expected Soviet ASW advances, a decision about whether the United States can live with fewer than 20 *Trident* submarines, and a consideration of options for increasing the size of the SSBN fleet permitted within START constraints. Because a large number of bomber weapons will be discounted under START, the airborne leg of the triad will be less constrained than either of the missile legs. Nevertheless, START will determine in large part the mix of stand-off and penetration bombers.

I suppose it is to be expected that, as we get closer to a START agreement, critics will sound the alarm that such large force reductions will put the US at a disadvantage relative to the USSR. Some, like Henry Kissinger, have blamed START for problems (such as ICBM vulnerability) that it did not create, and have overlooked the fact that the process of adapting US forces to the treaty may ultimately force some long-awaited solutions. It is pertinent to recall past alarms about windows of vulnerability, bomber and missile gaps, claims that the US was a second-class power in strategic weaponry and that the USSR was relentlessly outspending the United States in military programmes. I do not recall any of these charges being proved correct.

If and when an agreement is signed, Pentagon planners will be faced with a number of options – new and old – for tailoring the US triad to new specifications. What remains to be seen is whether the next Administration will seize the opportunity provided by START to work with the military and Congress to forge a new strategic consensus for the twenty-first century.

Guidelines for future endeavours
I would like to turn now to recommendations:
- As the process of reducing strategic forces gets under way, we should try to correct a mistake made in the 1970s: the decision to MIRV stra-

tegic missiles. Both sides would make a great contribution to strategic stability if they were to move towards single-warhead missiles. START will provide several incentives for doing so. This goal could be accomplished by removing all but a single warhead from existing MIRVed missiles, or by deploying a new single-RV system (such as *Midgetman* or *Minuteman IV*).
- Both sides would be wise to negotiate a package of 'predictability measures' to ensure the transparency of their ABM research and development activities. Both the United States and the Soviet Union have submitted versions of such a package at the Defense and Space Talks in Geneva. The US proposal includes annual briefings of the Soviet Union on planned SDI-related activities, visits to selected areas of missile defence laboratories and observation of SDI tests. The Soviet proposal includes data exchange on ABM programmes, meetings of experts, visits to test ranges, clarification of the obligations of both sides under the Treaty, on-site inspection, and consultations in the event that supreme national interests are threatened. The notion of a predictability package was conceived by the US to give the USSR 'half a loaf' while insisting on US freedom to follow a loose interpretation of the ABM Treaty. The Soviet Union accepts the idea of improved predictability, but would apply it to better verification of the strict interpretation of the ABM Treaty. If a new Administration abandons the loose interpretation and a predictability protocol is adopted, it would be in the interest of both sides.
- The United States and the Soviet Union should try to negotiate a total ban on ABM systems – another opportunity we failed to take in the 1970s. During SALT I, the Soviet Union in effect said 'make us a total ban offer', but President Nixon decided to reserve such a move for SALT II. Unfortunately, the matter was never raised again. If we could now negotiate a complete ban on the testing and deployment of ABM, the Soviet Union would dismantle its ineffective Moscow defence just as the US dismantled its *Safeguard* system in the mid-1970s. Research and development could continue. Above all, an ABM ban would make the strategic balance more stable and would remove the primary obstacle to deep reductions in offensive forces.
- The United States and the Soviet Union should try to clarify where they want arms control to lead. I believe that establishing a condition of minimum deterrence between the super-powers is a goal that should guide all present and future negotiations and unilateral measures. The goal of reducing strategic offensive forces to the lowest level at which a robust and stable deterrent can be maintained now seems to be gaining some respectability, even in military circles in Europe. Just what this level for stable force structures would be remains to be determined.
- Each side could do a great deal unilaterally to reduce its nuclear arsenal and the risk of accidental or inadvertent nuclear war. It is somewhat surprising to note how much US strategic forces have

changed since 1967 as a result of unilateral measures. As stated in the report of 'The Commission on Integrated Long-term Strategy' of January 1988, in 1967 the US had a third more nuclear weapons than we have today. The total explosive power of US nuclear weapons today is only one quarter of the peak reached in 1960. The average warhead yield today is only one quarter of the 1957 figure. Even on the Soviet side, while the total number of nuclear weapons has been increasing, the total explosive power and the average warhead yield have both been declining since the mid-1970s. This suggests that much can be done outside bilateral agreements to reduce the size and destructive power of the super-powers' nuclear arsenals. The sides could also take steps to improve command and control, and reduce the risk of miscalculation.

- The INF Treaty did not reduce the overall availability of fissionable materials for nuclear weapons, and neither will a START agreement. I think it is time to take another look at earlier US proposals for a cut-off of the production of fissionable material. A proposed production cut-off was essentially the first serious attempt at nuclear arms control. In 1982 the Soviet Union made a similar offer at the United Nations Second Special Session on Disarmament, but the US refused to discuss it.

Prospects

I would conclude by saying that these are troubled times for Americans, which may not augur well for early further progress in arms control. The United States is plagued with a myriad domestic doubts: about the White House's role in the Irangate fiasco, the integrity of the Justice Department leadership, how to handle astronomical trade and budget deficits, and, most recently, the whole military procurement effort. But with a new Administration, the great opportunities the START negotiations offer, and the passage of a little time, I think that these problems should not block a major improvement in Soviet-American relations. The case for larger reductions in deterrent forces is so strong that it should prevail in spite of our current domestic difficulties.

General Secretary Gorbachev, too, faces his own domestic difficulties. If he survives, and his more moderate policies prevail, the demonstrated Soviet interest in arms control can be expected to continue. Progress in negotiations, and any attendant easing of US-Soviet relations, will probably fortify the current belief in Europe that the risk of war is diminishing. This, in turn, could make moves to improve NATO's conventional forces more difficult and calls for US troop withdrawals more widespread. Both of these are developments to be guarded against. The US and its NATO allies must continue to improve their capabilities in Europe if the conventional force talks with the Warsaw Pact are to bear fruit and a stable peace is to be maintained.

We must plan for the long haul, as nuclear weapons will be with us for decades and there seems to be no panacea in sight. In so doing, we must remember that arms control is a slow, step-by-step process. It can make an enormous contribution to peace, but it can do little by itself: arms control alone cannot create stability, resolve conflict or reduce super-power tensions. Arms control can only be as effective as the larger national security policy of which it is a part.